Nannette Snow Emerson

A Thanksgiving Story

Nannette Snow Emerson

A Thanksgiving Story

ISBN/EAN: 9783744783095

Printed in Europe, USA, Canada, Australia, Japan

Cover: Foto ©Thomas Meinert / pixelio.de

More available books at **www.hansebooks.com**

A Thanksgiving Story;

EMBODYING

THE BALLAD

OF

"BETSEY AND I ARE OUT"

AND

OTHER POEMS,

BY

N. S. EMERSON.

NEW YORK:
G. W. Carleton & Co., Publishers.
LONDON: S. LOW & CO.
M.DCCC.LXXIII.

TO

MY MOTHER

(Who will Recognize every Actor in this Homely Drama)

I Dedicate My Book,

WISHING ONLY IT WERE BETTER WORTH

𝔗𝔥𝔢 𝔓𝔞𝔱𝔦𝔢𝔫𝔱 𝔞𝔫𝔡 𝔓𝔞𝔯𝔱𝔦𝔞𝔩 𝔓𝔢𝔯𝔲𝔰𝔞𝔩

THAT I KNOW

SHE WILL GIVE IT.

New York, 1873.

CONTENTS.

I.
	PAGE
THE STORY	9

II.
AUNT PRUDENCE'S STORY 38
[Odin's Boyhood.]

III.
COUSIN LUKE'S STORY 54
[Odin's Love Experience.]

IV.
UNCLE 'LIAB'S STORY 63
["Betsey and I are Out."]

V.
AUNT BETSEY'S STORY 71
[How Husband and I Made Up.]

VI.
UNCLE LUKE'S STORY 76
[Going to Channing's Meeting.]

VII.
COUSIN JOHN'S STORY 86
[In California.]

VIII.
UNCLE KING'S STORY 90
[Pat's Dream of Heaven.]

IX.
DEACON MUNROE'S STORY 94
[Church Discipline.]

X.

COUSIN NANNETTE'S STORY 100
[One Thanksgiving.]

XI.

COUSIN LAURETTE'S STORY . . . 118
[Will, My Brother.]

XII.

COUSIN TOM'S STORY. 123
[Youthful Experience.]

XIII.

AUNT MARGARET'S STORY 134
[The Octoroon.]

XIV.

LITTLE PHIL'S STORY 146
[A Legend of the Virgin.]

XV.

COUSIN NETTIE'S STORY 149
[Naming the Baby.]

XVI.

AUNT HEPZIBAH'S STORY 154
[That Mr. Reporter.]

XVII.

UNCLE NAT'S STORY 163
[Threescore Years.]

XVIII.

UNCLE CHRISTOPHER'S STORY 167
[Among the Mines.]

XIX.

COUSIN LAWRENCE'S STORY . . . 175
[The Christmas Gift.]

XX.

COUSIN KATE'S STORY 181
[Legend of the Waltzes.]

XXI.

COUSIN EMILY'S STORY 186
[The Temple of Vesta.]

I.

THE STORY.

'Tis Christmas eve! The snow is falling fast,
The sky is thick with clouds, that hurry by
Like chariots of midnight, wreathed in smoke;
And not a living thing is out o' doors.
Within, the firelight glows upon the hearth.
The ruddy hearth, with polished fire-dogs graced,
Shines yellower on the yellow-sanded floor,
Touches the tall, old-fashioned, cuckoo clock,
And lights the crook-necks, and the almanac,
Hung on a friendly beam, half out of sight.
Ah! blessed firelight, flickering through the room,
As if to compensate for lack of moon
And shining stars outside.
     We gather round,
While yet the candles stand unlighted near,
Like white-robed maidens, dainty, shy, and prim,
Until their crown of glory comes to bring
Life, usefulness, and martyrdom, and death.
Almost as strangers gather we, yet bound
By viewless cord of sympathy, or kin,
Or marriage covenant, which, more than tie
Of consanguinity, seems sacred now;
For we've been summoned from far-distant homes
On a strange errand.
     Listen, while I try
To make it plain to you, though this, I say,

That it is more like dreamland e'en to me,
Than sober, staid, New England verity.
There's Grandsire, in the chimney-corner wide,
And Grandma, nestled cosily beside,
In their two high-backed, wide-armed, oaken chairs,
That they have sat in almost every night
For more than sixty years.
      Grandma, for once,
Lets her thin hands lie idle in her lap
Without their knitting, and the 'customed click
Of swiftly-moving needles.
      Grandsire says,
That, fifty years ago, they filled those chairs
Plump full, from arm to arm ; but now they might
Both sit in one, and still have room to spare.
   For they are old, are very old indeed.
Oh, happy fate, to live so long on earth,
And bear such strong, fond, loving hearts through all.
Yet they have tasted sorrow, walked with grief,
And shrunk away from trouble oft, ere now.
Of their twelve children five have gone before
To faith's bright haven ; and the golden door
Swings lightlier on its hinges every time ;
And nearer draws the Heaven toward which they climb,
And brighter glows the star of hope, and still
More radiant burns the light on Zion's hill.
And six are living still—are here to-night.
I hear their voices talking o'er old times,
And soon they will be telling stories quaint,
And laughing at each other's kindly jests.
But one—alas ! we know not where he is ;
Or if the sea has 'whelmed him, or the strife
Of battle stricken out his changeful life.
We do not often talk of him. But now,

Just now, I cuddle down at Grandma's feet,
And, prompted, sometimes, by her gentle tones,
Will tell you of the children, one and all.
The eldest (Thomas) was a wild, bright boy,
For whose impatient spirit home seemed small;
And all the weary details of the farm
Were too much cost, and far too little gain.
Nor did he love his books. When sent to school
He ofttimes wandered off alone all day,
Through tangled wood, or by the river side,
Or drifting on his rude and treacherous raft,
O'er dangerous rapids and 'mid rocks and snags,
Down toward the sea.
     At twelve, he ran away,
And Grandma mourned as only mothers can.
Meanwhile the first twins, Mark and Martha, came,
And lived their little lives of four bright years,
And died, of fever, in a single night.
Then little Nathan, Grandma always said
He was a good boy—frolicsome, but kind,
And easy managed.
     He is here to-night.
His hair, like Grandsire's, almost snowy white;
But his fair, happy face, and bright gray eyes
Proclaim him always young.
     When he was twice
A twelvemonth, came wee Prudence, always quaint,
And wise, and womanly before her time.
I cannot think of her as of a wild
And merry-hearted girl, alive with mirth,
Laughing and dancing with the birds and flowers.
She never married, but just staid at home,
Caring for such grandchildren as were left
Like lambs without a fold.

But, oh, I wish
I could look in between the folded leaves
Of her shut heart, and find the golden core,
And read the deep, sweet romance hidden there.
No use! She seldom talks; and, good or ill
The wind may blow, she is Aunt Prudence *still*.
Before she reached her sober life's fourth year,
Another pair of twinnies drifted here,
Eliab and Eliza; and they lived,
And both were married one bright summer morn.
Eliab? Yes! He married Betsey Flint,
"Old Parson Flint's first gal," so Grandma says.
The aged parson died some years ago,
But Uncle 'Liab in the firelight sits,
His wife beside him and their Bessie near.
Eliza married Gregory Munroe—
"Deacon Munroe's one only precious son."
And Grandma never saw her face again,
After that wedding morning; for she died!
Lost with her brave young husband, on their way
From Afric's golden shore, where they had been
For five long years, upon their mission bent,
Teaching the dark-skinned children of the sun
The story of the gentle "Prince of Peace."
'Twas in the *Macedonia* that they sailed,
And she was wrecked, and many lives were lost,
They two among the number.
                            But their child,
Their one wee boy, scarce three years old, was saved.
The sailors cared for him and brought him home.
The rough old captain had been Grandsire's friend,
And so he took in tow the little craft,
And anchored him safe here at Ingleside.
His name was "Thomas Pratt Munroe," he said;

"Mamma had named him for her dear papa"—
And Grandma took him as a precious boon,
Left by her daughter, and thanked God for him.
I think too she was glad to hear his name;
It gave her an excuse for saying oft—
"Thomas, my boy," "Thomas, my child, be good."
But when those second twins were three years old,
Came Luke, then John; both grew to manhood's prime,
And John died suddenly, leaving one son,
Our cousin Luke, who always since has lived
At Ingleside. I hear him talking with
His Uncle Luke and Aunt Priscilla, now.
Their children, John, Priscilla, and Nannette,
Are with them. John, a dignified young man,
Has brought his pretty wife and baby boy.
Prissie is married, too; her little ones
Are sweet as sweetest blossoms—but Aunt Nan
Is just a good-for-nothing; people say;
She has no skill at housework—so she writes.

But then, when Uncle John was two years old,
Came stately Margaret; brown-eyed Patience next.
(She married young Squire Osborne, long ago,
And died, leaving one child—a fair, sweet girl,
Who since has married, and—they've just come in—
Captain and Mrs. Philip Brown—good friends,
And Philip's mother, old Aunt Hepsy Brown.)
And last, the warmest heart, the merriest laugh,
The most do-nothingness, that ever lurked
In one boy-mortal frame, came Christopher.
And now I've told you all the children's names,
Let us go back to Thomas, the first son.
For on his life and its strange incidents,
Hinges and turns our visit here to-night.

As Grandma says, when he was twelve years old
He ran away. And weary years crept by,
In which no word of tidings came from him.
And other boys grew up about the hearth,
But never from his mother's evening prayer
His name was missed.
    And when the nights were dark,
Or winds were high, or storms were beating wild,
She oft would press her face against the pane,
While the slow tears fell like a heavy rain,
And look out anxiously, and speak no word;
But then she prayed for him.
    Grandsire was stern
As kindly, in his moods. It hurt his pride
That his first-born should prove a lawless lad,
And though no doubt he often thought of him,
The name of Thomas never passed his lips.
But one cold, stormy, drifting, Christmas eve
(That might have been a prototype of this)
They heard a sound of voices in the yard,
Strong, hearty voices, merry laughter too,
And stamping of great boots, and shaking off
Of clinging snow from caps and coats, and then
The old shed-door swung on its leathern hinge,
And in the wanderer strode.
    His mother knew,
At the first glance, the boy who erst had lain
Upon her breast, and drawn his life from thence;
And while the others wondered who had come,
She fell atween his strong and muscular arms,
And kissed his face, and kissed his happy eyes,
And laughed and cried, and said, "My child," "My boy."
Then Grandsire rose and stretched a trembling hand
Toward him who had been lost and now was found,

And tried to make his voice sound calm and firm,
To speak the one word—" Thomas."
                              Out it came,
Bearing the pardon which the truant one
Had never thought to ask, and freighted full
Of faith, forgiveness, hope, and welcome home.
It must have been a rare and goodly sight,
To see those two, long-severed, sire and son,
Meet and clasp hands across the vanished years,
In which the sire had grown to middle age,
The son from boy to manhood.
                              Then, full soon,
The shy-eyed little ones were taken up,
And kissed and called by the familiar names,
And all miscalled.
                    For John was little Nat,
And baby Margaret was little Prue,
And who that tall young fellow (Nathan) was,
He could not even guess.
                         But while all eyes
And hearts and thoughts were fixed on brother Tom,
A stranger stood unnoticed at the door.
Prudy was first to see and speak to him;
She said, "My brother is so much engrossed
With home and parents, and the young folks there,
He does not heed his friend. But come you in,
For his sake you will find a welcome warm."
And the fair stranger, with his ruddy cheeks,
And locks of tawny gold, and blue bright eyes,
Laughed out, and said, "My heart is full of glad
To see such happy. I forgot myself.
But you—you call him brother; he has told
Me, when we lay upon the frozen deck,
Counting the cold, white stars, or when we built

Our camp-fires on the snow, and wolves' eyes gleamed
About among the shadows, then, in talk,
He told me of his home, his mother dear,
His small, young brother, and a younger girl;
And, sometimes, he would heave a sigh, and say,
'I wonder if the little Prue can sing,
And if she talks of me or speaks my name?
No, no! they will not teach her that,' he said;—
And can it be you are that little girl?"
'Tween smiles and blushes Prudence answered him
(Though half abashed at his admiring gaze
And his frank boyishness): "I must, I think,
Be the same little Prue of whom he talked;
But I cannot remember when he left;
And now I've grown so very large and tall,
He does not know or think of me at all."
Then Thomas turned and sought his friend, and said
Some words in foreign speech (they knew not what),
And then he led him forward to the group,
Who watched him silently, and said to them,
By way of introduction: "This is he
Who saved my life in the far Northern sea,
And risked his own, and won this ugly scar,
That, lacking gentle treatment, serves to mar
His brow's fair beauty. This is my one friend!
His name, Eric Fitzeric, and a goodly name
In his own country, where the snow lies white
Nine-twelfths the year."

     And Grandsire greeted him
With kindly words, and Grandma clasped his hand,
And all the yonkels laughed to see him laugh,
And wondered why the tears should fill his eyes
When he was happy.

     That wild Christmas eve

Was full of joy; and long ere light, next morn,
The air was ringing with the children's shouts,
Their merry shouts that would not be repressed;
The sun came up, and looked his benison
Upon the white-robed earth;
      The farmers drove
A long team through the drift-encumbered roads,
Adding another yoke of restless steers
Or patient oxen from each farm-house yard,
As they drew near it, heralded by calls
Of "Merry Christmas!" from the crowd of boys
Who slipped and balanced on the tilting logs
Chained to the clumsy sled.
      Nathan and Luke
Were out with Buck and Star at the first sound
Of distant echo from the coming throng.
And soon the curious news was circled round,
That Squire Pratt's Thomas had come home again,
Alive and well. And many hurried in
To offer words of welcome and good cheer;
And Grandsire gave them cider and hot flip,
And looked the proud and happy man he was.
But Thomas and the stranger, Eric, drew
The light sleigh out, and hitched the colts to it,
And just as they were ready for a start,
Thomas called out, "Say, Mother, would you like
A drive to Salem? We are going down
To bring our sea traps home. We wo'nt be long!"
And Eric whispered, "Ask the little Prue."
But Mother quick made answer: "Are you wild,
To think of driving, such a day as this,
Ten blessed miles o'er these half-trodden roads?"
And Thomas laughed, and said,
      "If we should fail

To make our way, we'll leave the little sledge,
And taking each a horse up in our arms,
We'll travel on with them."
                                And with one snap,
And flourish of a long, lithe whip, that made
The boys' eyes shine with envy, off they went.
Soon, as they promised, they were back again,
And, oh! the wondrous store of foreign things
Those wondrous chests contained. For there were hid
All kinds of fishing-tackle, nets, and seines,
Flies, poles, floats, bobs and sinkers, cords and reels,
Lines, jointed rods, bright signals, spears and coys,
That set the boys half-wild with dreams of sport,
And vague, bewildering plans and rude device
For lighting fires and fishing through the ice.
Then there were bear-skins, shaggy, coarse, and black,
White wolf skins, fine as fleece, and soft as snow,
And garments strangely fashioned; bows and clubs,
That, sometime, in their rude way, must have served
As implements of warfare or defence;
And pictures of strange people; branching horns,
From the wild mountain goat, and rare, bright shells—
That Grandma, with all praiseful reverence, called
"Beautiful dust from off the Great One's feet"—
And skins of snakes, and fishes, and stuffed birds,
And bits of coral, and brown, sunny cones
That grew on tall Norwegian pines, that nod
Above eternal snows.
                        The house was like
A museum to the quiet village folk,
For years thereafter. Aye! and even now
Are many traces left of all that gave
That queer collection its strange interest.

But that wild winter marked an era bright
In the whole village.
            Each would vie with each
In merry-andy pulls, and sewing-bees,
And junketings, that seemed to seek to make
The time pass lightly for the strangers twain
Who sojourned there.
            And Thomas and his friend
Were always ready for the merriest sport,
The maddest frolic, and the keenest mirth;
Sometimes they wore their monstrous fur-topped boots,
And danced quaint, awkward dances, and sang songs
In foreign dialect.
            And Eric taught
The little Prue to sing, and dance with him
In wild, fantastic measure, clicking out
The time with ivory castanets, and oft
Striking her brazen heels, and ringing soft
The tiny silver bells that hung upon
The Polish boots he gave her.
            I have seen,
Hidden away, in an old trunk, upstairs,
Those same old boots, yellow and faded now,
But once blue satin, laced with silver cord,
And edged with eider.
            But the young men oft
Journeyed away for days, sometimes for weeks,
To distant cities, studying laws, and rules,
And forms of government, and different ways
Of settling and arranging troublous points.

Spring came at last, with tardy feet and slow,
And winter gathered up his robe of snow,
And walked away to hide on some far hill,

Whence often his hoarse breathing, loud and chill,
Would fright the violets and snowdrops pale,
As they looked up and trembled in the vale.

Came also letters, covered all outside
With postmarks that betrayed their wanderings wide,
And the young men held confabs long and low,
And Grandma's heart asked sadly, " Must they go ? "
Thomas went first, while the March winds were blowing,
And gave no reason for his sudden going.

But while he journeyed, letters often came,
Mostly to Eric. He would read them o'er,
And say, " Now I must go to-morrow sure."
And still "to-morrow," and "to-morrow," then,
Like one who dreads to leave a cosey nook,
And battle with the world.
      Once he did start,
And rode away toward a near sea-port town,
And hurried back, and flung himself full length
Upon the floor, like some too-petted child,
And hid his tearful face in Grandma's lap,
And moaned, " Oh, save me, save me from my fate ! "
And Grandma said, " You are a brave, good boy;
If you have troubles you have borne them well,
Nor burdened others with their weary weight.
But if without betraying any trust,
Or breaking any pledge or confidence,
You can talk freely, tell me what it is
That troubles you so sadly.
      I have seen
The bitten lip, the tightly closéd hand,
And heard the words half uttered, half repressed,

Yet could not offer sympathy the while
You asked not for it."
                    Then he answered her :
"Oh, mother, I am sad and full of grief;
I am a Norman! and I love my home,
My country, with a Norman's honest love ;
But I have no desire to rule, no love of power,
And all my father's high, ambitious plans
I cannot share.
                "When I was ten years old,
They carried me to Paris to a school,
And one long year I staid there ;
                        "Then news came
That I might make one leetle visit home.
I went, and found—how can I tell it you,
Who, breathing always the free, bracing air
Of a Republic, cannot understand
The small, small turmoils and perpetual strife
That aggravate a monarchy?
                        " I found
My precious mother, weary, sick, and sad,
And father, burdened with affairs of state,
Full of ambitious plans, and most for me.
The Bonaparte was moving, and the souls
Of all our people had been deeply stirred;
And I—boy as I was—I was betrothed
To one whom I had never seen before,
A woman thrice my age, and forty times
My overmatch in world experience,
In deep and cunning craft that moves the world ;
My heart turned sick within me, when I looked
Upon her dark French face, and saw the lines
Of diplomatic strategy and skill,
And all the whirlpool of ambition there.

My father is a ruler. Every word
He uttered was a law from that hour forth.
And when I gladly would have pleased myself
With boyish sports, or nestled down in peace
Beside my mother, entertaining her
With stories of my school life, boyish themes,
Or listening to the legends, quaint and old,
She knew so well, about the Vikings bold,
Who sailed the frosty Norland seas about,
Clad all in seal-skins, then his iron will
Held me to do his bidding ; and, with him,
I passed through some strange ceremonial,
That made me chosen ruler by the laws,
And made me, too, the promised spouse and lord
Of that old witch.

"Then, when they took me back
To school again, I—yes—I ran away."
"Oh, child!" I can imagine Grandma's voice,
Plaintive and gentle in its chiding tones,
"Oh, child, my boy ! why did you run away?"
Then his eyes brightened, and his breath came quick.
"It was the sea," he said, "the beautiful sea ;
She lures me so I cannot say her nay ;
When I was yet a little dimple boy,
She used to run far up the shining sand,
And kiss my bare brown toes, and draw her hair
About my ankles, and slip back again,
And toss her white arms up and call to me.
And when first time I crept alone, unseen,
Into a boat, drawn high upon the sand,
The sea laughed out, and sang a song of joy,
And came and stirred the boat with gentle hand,
And lifted it and let it down again,

And rocked it lightly, laughing all the time,
While I laughed back, in answer.
       "Soon she grew
Stronger, and sucked the barque from off the beach,
And launched it fairly out among the rocks.
Just then I thought of mother;
       "Thought if she
Should see me there, that she would surely die,
And 'twould be I that killed her.
      "So I prayed,
'Oh, pretty sea, if you will take me home,
And not let mother know what I have done,
I'll grow to be a man, and build for you
A monstrous ship, and call her only "*Thanks*,"
And give her to you for your very own,
To be your plaything for a hundred years.'
I thought the sea was angry, for she gave
The boat a push among the jagged rocks,
And it stuck fast, and threw me on my face,
Just as my careless nurse appeared in sight,
And would have rushed into the boiling surf,
And waded out to me waist-deep, save that
A fisher lad, her lover, drew her back,
And came for me himself, and took me up
In his wet arms, and bore me safely home.
And mother knew not, till long afterward,
The story of my peril.
     "But I felt
That I had made a covenant with the sea,
And often walking on the rocky shore
I whispered, '*Thanks*,' and often murmured o'er
My promise that I never might forget.
But as I said before, I ran away,
And went to sea, when I was twelve years old.

Wrecked on the coast, the *Penguin* picked us up,
And there I found your Thomas.
       We were both
Mere truant schoolboys, sadly out of place
Before the mast, and both (we liked to think)
Made for advancement, and for better things.
We clung together as year followed year,
And taught each other all each other knew,
And often talked of home and mother-love.
At last we made a compact, and agreed
That he should go to Norway, home with me,
And stay a year; and then that we should both
Come to America, and here, perhaps,
If we could be contented, on dry land,
Make us a home, and settle down and live
Together. . For I longed to read the laws
That gave equality to every man,
And let the people choose their rulers just.

We went to Norway. It was when the death
Of that great masterpiece of selfishness,
The Bonaparte, was heralded as news,
And told from lip to lip, from land to land.
But still our own home troubles had not ceased,
And there were rumors of impending wars.
Sweden was murmuring like a wind-swept wood,
Prussia was shrinking from approaching fate.
But dear old Norway held, with swerveless grip,
Her constitution, and the rights it gave.
My precious mother, for whose sake alone
I had returned, was lying very ill.
They said I could not see her, but she knew,
By some quick instinct, that her boy was near,
And bade them haste to call me to her side.

Long time we talked, she lying in my arms,
And blessing me with every feeble breath,
And telling me how patient I must be
With father, in the future.
                         For her sake,
I promised not to quarrel with his will;
And lingering on, hour after hour, she seemed
To live but in my presence.
                         Oft she said,
'I knew God would be kind to me at last,
And let me see my darling once again,
Before mine eyes were closed forever, or
My heart had ceased to beat.'
                         And so she lay,
And breathed her happy, happy life away,
And left me desolate.
                         Oh, in that hour
How deeply did I pray to follow her,
To lie down in a calm and dreamless sleep,
Close at her side; or, if the soul can live
After its mortal garb is lain aside,
To go with her to our Nirvana blest,
And there drink deeply from the fount of peace.

But there was father, scarcely giving time
To decorous burial of his saintly wife,
Then hurrying back to business.
                         He was glad
To have me there just then, to carry out
Some plan of his; and so, when the great bells
Were scarce done tolling, they were bade to ring
A merry peal for my approaching bridal.

I heard the edict, and I hurried out

From the gray castle walls I so abhorred,
And said to Thomas, 'Let us leave to-night;
I cannot bring my conscience to endure
This senseless mockery.'
      But Thomas said,
'You promised your dear mother, now in heaven,
That you would not oppose your father's will.'
And while we talked my father came that way,
Walking with slow, uncertain, troubled steps.
I saw, or thought I saw, on his stern brows
The traces of a conflict and a grief
Beyond all telling.
      When he spoke, his voice
Was low but earnest, and he said to us,
'Boys, would you like to go to sea again?'
I answered, 'If it please you, Sire, I think
I'd like to visit foreign countries more,
And learn the laws that govern them, before
I take my place as guide or ruler here.'
Then father's voice dropped lower as he said,
'It shall be so, my boy. I do not wish
To be, or e'en to seem, a cruel sire!
If I have erred, it hath been for thy sake,
For I have only planned, and hoped, and wrought,
That every plan and hope might be fulfilled
In thy young life.
      My boy, my froward boy,
Why canst thou not take up, with hearty will,
The office I am ready to resign,
And give our people what they now most need,
A friendly ruler and a ruling friend.'

In penitent and sorry zeal, I said,
'My sire, I will. Henceforth, my only thought

Shall be the keeping of our Norland home
In peace with all the world, and strong and firm
In her own safety.
     " 'I will study well
Her wants and needs, and lay aside all dreams
Of selfish happiness, or love, or fame.'
And then he spoke again, as though the words
Must come, and shamed him with their bitter power.
'Thy bridal? Shall it be deferred for yet
A little while? Or shall the bells ring on?'
Then springing up in savage, quick revolt,
My soul arose and struck him through my eyes;
And then, at his keen look of proud distress,
Sank back abashed, and plead in silent woe.

And Thomas broke the awkward pause that fell
Like heavy cloud atween us.
     'Honored Sire,
You asked us would we like to go to sea;
Have you a plan for us?'
     'We have a plan,'
My sire made answer. 'We will tell it you,
And if you have aught better to propose,
We will consider your proposal then.
My plan is, that the appointed bridal-hour
Be not deferred. But that the grand old house
Of Dauphin Bassompierre thus lend its strength
To the young pride of our Fitzeric, now;
And when the rites are o'er, the papers signed,
Then if you wish to go abroad again
We'll not deter you.
     " 'For a single year
You can return to the old boyish life,
Still bearing with you, wheresoe'er you go,

The thought, the purpose you have just expressed,
To keep before your mind and in your heart,
The good of Norway.'
      "So the bells rang on,
And people gathered from the hamlets near,
Half sad, half sullen, wholly without hope,
And well-nigh ready for revolt or war,
But keeping up the mockery of joy,
The ghost of revelry."
      Then hot tears came
And dripped a quiet shower on Grandma's hands,
And the blue eyes burned strangely, and the voice
Fell to a hoarse, low whisper, as he said:
"And I was married!
      "Ah, you free-born folk,
Who love and hate at will, and choose your friends,
And choose your work, and set your price for it,
And wed because you love, and if the love
Wears out, as all earth's perishable things
May do, through time and trouble, then you find
In your own lives and laws some mete return
For every wrong and sorrow—little you
Can know of all the bitterness that lies
Beneath the gilded chains, the hopeless forms,
And senseless rituals, that go to give
Strength to our feudal government.
      "But I
Was glad, at any price, to win again
My freedom for a year. Thus was I wed;
And then we hurried off, and pleasant days
We dallied through upon the deep blue sea.
The storms were only pastimes to our ken;
The calms were long delicious hours of rest,
For we were free.

"At last, when half our year
Of holiday had passed, we drifted here;
A new world opened to my wondering eyes.
I thought, in Paris, I had grown blasé,
Boy, as I was, and weary of the world.
But like a strange, sweet problem, hard to solve,
Yet well worth solving, seemed you Yankee folk.
Un-French, un-English—true American—
Brave, frugal, self-respectful, fond of home;
And every one, man, matron, maid and youth,
Eager to learn.

"I have been happy here;
So happy, mother, that I quite forget
The bitter past. But it will all come back
Keener and bitterer, far, than ever, now,
For I must go. From day to day there come
Letters and messages that bid me haste.
Oh, mother! save me—save me from my fate—
You have been kind to me! O, hide me here,
And let me stay with you and little Prue."

Then Grandma smoothed the tangled, tawny hair,
And said—"Be brave, my boy—to you is given
A solemn trust which you must ne'er neglect.
You are a ruler! For your Norland home
You must give up all petty, selfish plans,
And let your people feel that they can trust,
And lean upon you.

"Build yourself a name
Worthy all generous and abiding faith.
If you have learned aught from our simple ways
Of ministering justice, heed it well;
And when your father to your care resigns
The office he has held, is holding now,

Bear ye it nobly for his noble sake.
And, Eric, more than this : do you forget
You are a husband? Wrong as it may be
To marry without love, the vow once breathed
Should ne'er be lightly held, or lain aside.
Go home to Norway. To your mother's home.
For her sake prove yourself a worthy son,
A faithful ruler, and a husband true ;
Remember always that she waits for you,
Just out of sight, but never far away.
That, though she may not know what changeful path
Your weary feet are walking, or what work
Your hands have chosen, she will always know
If you have kept your heart pure, and have tried
To do your duty.
    "Let me thank you now,
For all your kindness to my wandering boy,
The faithful brother-love that brought you here
And made you seem as one of us.
      "You know
My blessing will go with you where you go,
And I shall aye be glad to hear from you."

Then there were farewells spoken, sad and low,
And eyes unused to tears were strangely dim,
And sobs were smothered, and the stranger boy
Went out from that bright home as drifts a ship
From some safe harbor far upon the sea,
To battle with the winds that bear it on
And waves that beat against it.
      For a time
Letters came often from the truant lads,
Telling how Eric reached his Norway home,
And there met Thomas ; and how oft they talked

Of dear New England, and the loved ones there.
Then came the news of trouble in the state,
Of revolution threatened, and revolt;
And then the letters stopped.
                         Months grew to years,
And crept along their uneventful way;
But Grandma was not forced to bear again
The ban of silence added to her grief.
For oft the name of Thomas found a place
In Grandsire's evening prayers; and sometimes, too,
He prayed for blessings on "Our absent ones."
And then she thought of Eric, and her lips
And heart gave echo to the formal words
That seemed to bring God's kindness near to her.

Three times a twelvemonth!
                         Grandma wished sometimes
She could not count the lagging days so well.
No word had reached her from her absent boys;
But one fair morning in the early spring
A stranger to the gray old farm-house came,
Wearing the garb of a seafaring man,
A rough frieze jacket, and big, fur-topped boots,
That made the children stop him, to inquire—
"Have you a brother Eric?"   "Is he well?"
"And will he soon again come home to us?"
The sailor did not heed them. On he strode,
Up to the kitchen door, and entered in,
And dropped a clumsy bundle on the floor.
The burden shook itself and fell apart,
And out came, like a chicken from its shell,
A live boy baby, with a little head
All covered o'er with tangled flaxen hair,
Two blue, bright eyes, a ruddy, dimpled face,

Plump, sturdy limbs, and frock of ragged fur.
The little fellow laughed and rubbed his eyes,
Then, seeing the strange faces, pouted out
A grieved and quivering lip, and 'gan to cry.
Aunt Prudence took the stranger baby up,
And kissed his brown, pink face, and smoothed his hair;
And he, well pleased with all her gentle care,
Nestled his head against her sheltering arm,
And cooed contentedly, while Grandsire strove
To learn whence came the stranger, and what meant
His broken speech, and what the news he bore.
Two words of English only could he speak,
"Thomas" and "Baby." But by gestures swift,
And sounds more eloquent than any words,
He made them understand that there had been
A battle on the land, a wreck at sea,
And from the shattered débris he had caught
This little waif, and found upon his back
A package wrapped in parchment, bound about,
And sealed with many seals.
      Upon its face
Was written, in a clear, bold English hand
(Though stained and faded by the salt sea waves),
The Country, State, and Town, and Grandsire's name.

They gave the rugged sailor food and rest.
And then he went away, leaving a kiss
On the wee baby's either dimpled cheek.
With trembling hands, that quite belied the look
Of stern, forced calmness, on his eager face,
Grandsire made careful haste to cut the cords
That bound the curious packet; and within
He found two long, strange letters, written o'er

With foreign words, and signed with foreign names,
But on them both he recognized no more
Of meaning than was hidden or expressed
In the plain English name of "Thomas Pratt."
Still o'er and o'er he turned the mystic things,
And pondered long, and yet learned nothing new.

The baby staid, perforce, and cooed and laughed,
And cried plain English; but the few strange words
His young lips spoke were only Greek to them.
    When evening came he clasped his dimpled hands,
And looking upward to the solemn stars,
With eyes as solemn, murmured broken sounds,
And 'mong them, oft-repeated, full of grave
And reverent meaning, they could understand
The one word "Odin." It might mean, perchance,
Or "Sire," or "Mama," or his own sweet name;
But though he soon was christened "Thomas Pratt,"
The children always called him Odin. Soon
He came to know and answer to this name,
At first with wondering looks, and half-abashed;
Then laughing light as seeming to enjoy
The half-familiar sound.
                    So time passed on.
The little stranger throve and grew, and held
A warm, bright corner in that formal home,
Where each one loved him.
                    When he went to school
The stern-faced teacher bade him tell his name.
He had been taught, as country children are,
The formula of name and age, as part
Of that inquisitorial device
Yclept the Shorter Catechism.

                        But he
Forgot it all in the new strangeness there,
And said—" My name is Odin."
                        Down it went
Upon the teacher's book—just "Odin Pratt,"
And so from that time forth they never tried
To call him aught beside.
                        A score of years
Went by and Odin found his share of all
The ups and downs, and ins and outs of life;
More than a common share, perhaps; but when
They thought he was content to settle down
And stay at home in peace and quietness,
And study medicine, as he commenced,
And grow ambitious, in a way, perchance,
And, by and by, do something grand and great,
Then he with Helen Winthrop fell in love.
For many years the Winthrops and the Pratts
Had held a bitter and unreasoning feud;
Commencing first, I think, in that some Pratt
Had joined the Baptists, in the early time,
When Baptist-whipping was a legal sport,
And some old Winthrop being then in power,
Had flayed the culprit with unholy zeal.
Since then the foolish jealousies of pride
Had kept a formal coolness, passing down
From sire to son. The women folks had tried
To overlook the trouble and be friends.
But stern New England men are not to lay
The great first principles of strife aside
For any woman's effort. So Squire Pratt
Held his back stiff, and good Squire Winthrop bowed;
And neither spoke, without some grand excuse.
Poor Odin must have known this trouble well,

But he forgot or quite ignored it all,
And went his frank, straight-forward, earnest way,
Until he found himself wronged and abused;
Aunt Prudence knows it all.—She soon will tell
It, like a story, if we wait to hear.
But be it how it may, I only know
Odin left suddenly, and went away.

He had been gone three months ere we received
A single line to tell what way he went.
Then came a letter, written on ship-board,
And he was bound for Norway.
       Three months more
And came another letter, plain and brief,
Yet thridded with a jubilant undertide,
Which one must know our Odin long and well
To understand.
     "Call all hands home," it said.
"Set all the chimneys roaring with great fires,
And I'll be with you ere the midnight bells
Ring in the glory of the Christmas morn,
And peace and good-will once again are born."
The summons crept about from one to one,
And each one "Rather guessed it would not pay
To go a-'histing round—'twas always cold
At Christmas-time;——true, all the crops were in,
There was not much to do—but then—but then—"
The fact is, reader, we're a homely clan,
With very little romance in our lives;
Silver and golden wedding-days go by,
And every kind of anniversary;
Yet nothing ever served to draw us back
Together to the old home nest, till this
Wild bugle-call echoed across the sea,

And, answering to its summons,—here we are.
Though each one "Rather guessed it would not pay
To come," yet each one came.
                          From the far coast
Of California Cousin Tom Munroe
Has brought a heart as merry as a boy
Ten summers old. From Colorado comes
Uncle Luke's John, bringing his wife and child.
Ohio sends us kindly Uncle Nat,
With his two children, Kate, and Cousin Nat,
(His wife has long since passed away from earth.)
While up from Squam drives jolly Uncle Kit,
With sweet Aunt Minnie, and their bright-faced girl,
Laurette. They have a son, too, but he went
Away out West, more than a year ago.
They did expect him home last fall, but, now,
They have not told me why he did not come.
'Twas Cousin Tom who welcomed Uncle Kit
With, "So you thought you'd navigate this way?
Well, get inside and warm your frozen toes;
Deacon Munroe is there, and all the rest;
You'll find them playing euchre or old sledge;
Give them my compliments, and they'll be sure
To find a place for you beside the board."
Then Uncle Christopher shook his long whip,
And tried to give the merry rogue a cut,
While dear Aunt Prue with her severest tone
Said, "Tom, I am ashamed! For, I declare,
You do worse credit to your bringing up
Than any boy I ever took in hand."
"Now, Prudence, Prudence," Tom began again,
Mimicking Grandmother's reproving tone,
"Don't let me hear another word from you;
The Deacon is a relative of mine."

And still the guests keep coming—every kith
And kin has been invited, with their friends,
And all their friends' friends. But the house is large
And help is plenty. And Aunt Prudence knows
Which nook or corner every one can fill.
Aunt Margaret and her husband came, last night,
Most unexpectedly from Washington.
He is a Congressman; and who could think
That they would leave the whirl of social life
At the gay Capital in winter-time,
To spend the holidays at Ingleside?
Grandsire I know is very proud of them—
"My son, Judge King; my daughter, Mrs. King."
How often I have heard him try to hide
The conscious tone and accent in his voice
When introducing them.

      But long ago
I promised you a story from Aunt Prue.
Now listen; very soon you'll hear her tell,
To twice a score of young folks gathered in
The sitting-room, the story of her boy.

II.

AUNT PRUDENCE'S STORY.

[ODIN'S BOYHOOD.]

Now, children, you know I'm no poet;
    But sometimes the world seems so fair,
My thoughts set themselves, half unconscious,
    To a changeful and rhythmical air.
And thus they slip down on the paper,
    A kind of a journal; and so
I'll read to you all about Odin,
    Who came to our home long ago.

One year, when the May flowers were lifting
    Each pink-white, pale face from the sod,
And the Bobolinks and Orioles were calling
    "Praise God in the highest, praise God,"
A shy little flaxen-haired stranger
    Found shelter within our home nest,
Like some tiny birdling, storm-beaten,
    Dropped down to a haven of rest.

We found him a wonderful treasure;
    He was petted and loved and caressed,
And in caring for him in his weakness,
    All the household seemed brightened and blest.
He told us no sweet baby story
    Of why he was left so alone,
Nor parent nor friend came to claim him,
    So they gave him to me for my own.

In joy and gladness year followed year,
But a fearful hour for my boy drew near;
The terrible scourge of childhood came
With masque of scarlet and breath of flame.
It stole the life from his ruddy blood,
And filled his heart with a molten flood;
Poured a tide of fire through each knotted vein,
And touched with fever his burning brain.

Down, down to the brink of the river of death,
With weakened pulses and bated breath,
Where wild delirium painted still
His horrible phantoms with fearful skill,
Till, the bounds of consciousness reached and passed,
My boy was afloat 'mong the shades, at last.

He heard us mourning beside his bed,
Yet he could not tell us he was not dead;
His hands lay folded, his eyes were sealed,
No tell-tale heart-throb his life revealed.
We bore him away to the churchyard green;
You cannot believe it, 'tis like a dream.
We paused in silence beside his bier;
He has told me since he could plainly hear
The words of the Pastor, low and clear,
Telling the mourners in God to trust,
And murmuring solemnly, "Dust to dust."

Poor Odin, still tranced in that breathless sleep,
Felt his strength fail slowly, and still and deep
Despair was settling upon his soul.
But the sexton was feeble and very old;
He had loved the boy with the winsome face,
Who lay in that narrow resting-place,

And the hot tears came to his dim gray eye,
As over and over he wondered why
The old live on, and the young must die!

He could not fasten the coffin lid,
The tools he was holding slipped and slid—
A sudden crash, and a crimson streak
Stained brow and temple and pallid cheek.
Two eyes flashed open, the pale lips stirred,
And the frightened sexton with terror heard
A moan of pain;—then—I cannot tell
How the next hour passed, but the fearful spell
Was broken at last, and at close of day,
Weak, but conscious, our darling lay,
Not in the night of the noisome tomb,
But hushed to sleep in the twilight gloom
Of his own dear dream-haunted, pleasant room.

Up from his couch, as by magical power,
Odin grew stronger with each passing hour;
Out in the world with its busy train
Soon he was taking his place again.
What could be freer from cares and fears,
Than life for him with his twice seven years?

Fourteen! Oh venturesome, heyday hour
Of youth, scarce conscious of manhood's power,
Yet turning with smile of ineffable scorn
From the toys and treasures of childhood's morn.

Fourteen—and the world had a charming look,
More tempting by far than his dull school-book.
I saw how impatient and restless he grew
As health and vigor came back; but I knew

He never would leave us to run away,
So I watched him anxiously day by day.

Day by day, as the weeks crept on,
Month by month, till three years had gone;
Then Father came home from the seaport town,
That lay below us all gray and brown,
And said (and I fancied his face looked pale),
" In four days more will the *Kepler* sail."

I never knew by what trick or plan
He gained the consent of that grave, stern man;
But soon our Odin, still strong and free
At heart, found the place where he longed to be,
A sailor, afloat on the broad, blue sea.

He stood on the deck of the outward-bound,
The winds and waters sang pæans around,
The shore receded; and if some tears
Dimmed his loving eyes, and some homesick fears
Lay deep in his heart, as he thought with pain
Of the friends he never might see again;
Yet he would not turn from his chosen way;
He was too earnest to pause or stay.

He learned to cling to the giddy shroud
When the winds were piping fierce and loud,
And he never shrank from the swaying mast
When the blinding sleet was driving fast
O'er the slippery deck, and the Captain's voice
Rose high and hoarse 'bove the tempest's noise.

  * * * * * *

Then dawned the glory of tropical skies;
He saw from the waters the Southern Cross rise.

Green grew the shores of that fair foreign land,
Bright in the sunshine was gleaming the sand.

Strange, dusky forms flitted forward and fro,
Friendliest greeting they came to bestow.

Rarest-hued blossoms and rich-fruited trees
Shook down their tribute with each passing breeze.

Oh 'twas a blessing no landsman can ken,
Just to enjoy terra-firma again.

Lying all night 'mong the shadowy vines,
Sipping the fruit-juices sweeter than wines.

Roaming abroad, ere the fierce god of day
Burned the faint breath of the spices away.

Fearless of danger his path often turned
Through jungle grasses where tiger eyes burned.

And without dreaming of caution or fear,
One day he passed a fierce tigress so near,

Almost her breath scorched his feet as he trod,
Marking her footprints along the fresh sod.

But gorged with the blood of a wild goat, she lay
Too lazy to lift her huge paw for more prey.

Time came at last when Odin knew
That deep within his nature grew
  One wish that would not die.
He longed to see his home once more,
To tread the old, familiar shore,
To clasp the hands he clasped of yore,
  And meet some loving eye.

For he had garnered golden store,
  With all the simple savage lore
    Which that free life could teach;
Had launched with them the frail canoe,
Had gathered gems of rarest hue,
    And learned their curious speech.

Until that very freedom came
  To haunt him like a spectre flame
    That burns without consuming.
And so he bade them all farewell,
Each balmy breeze and palmy dell,
To seek again the chilling night,
Where northern stars were burning bright,
    And northern frost-flowers blooming.

He trod again the vessel's deck,
He saw his island home, a speck,
  Fade in the distance dim.
The world of waters widened round,
Far to the dark horizon's bound.
The mermaid sang with lulling sound,
  And brought new life to him.

But oh! what pen has power to trace
Each varying phase of nature's face,

Upon the wide, wide sea.
The listless calm day after day;
The burning sunbeams as they lay,
Like fiery arrows falling fine
Above the strange equator line;
The round red sun, with bronze-dark face,
Slow rolling through its breathless space;
The wondrous phosphorescent light
That turns the sea to fire at night;
The long, deep, undulating swell;
The rising breeze, that comes to tell
The calm is over; and the gray
Horizon, stretching far away,
Where, like a boat at anchor, lay
A small dark cloud with edge of snow.
Ah! looking on it who could know
That, lurking in that filmy cloud,
A demon strove to weave a shroud
For Odin in the sea.

The voyage was almost o'er at last;
It seemed the dangers all were passed;
They saw beneath the sunset skies
The distant shores of home arise,
And said, "If but the morn is bright
"We'll anchor ere to-morrow night."
But soon the winds howled like a pack
Of hungry hounds, let loose to track
Some flying fugitive; and high
The fierce waves rose against the sky;
And on the good ship hurried fast,
A helpless thing before the blast,
And labored on the laboring sea,
Like chainèd monster, to be free.

The reef-points rattled on the sail,
That shivered in the fearful gale.
The sailors heard the water-sprite,
Muttering of wreck, the live-long night,
And caught above the tempest's roar,
The sound of breakers on the shore.
Near, nearer, came that fearful sound,
High, higher, rose the waves around,
Keen, keener, cut the driving sleet,
Swift, swifter yet, and yet more fleet,
With helm, and sail, and rudder gone,
The good ship *Kepler* hurried on;
Until, with one terrific shock,
She struck upon a sunken rock.

Over the deck the great waves rolled,
And every shrieking timber told
Its story of defiance bold.
But mate and captain lay,
Stricken as by a single blow,
Senseless and breathless, lying low;
The sailors bore them down below,
    And helpless turned away.

Then Odin raised his boyish face,
Where not the keenest eye could trace
One line of doubt or fear.
He knew how slight their chance must be
For safety on that boiling sea,
And yet he manned the minute-gun,
Calmly, as though the setting sun
Shone over waters clear.
Perhaps his young heart faltered, when
He saw those sun-browned, stern-browed men,

Look with despair athwart the skies,
And then into each other's eyes,
With silent, long farewell.
But aye, his steady eye and lip
Said still, "We wont give up the ship."
And so, until the early dawn,
Those signals of distress boomed on,
Like some grand funeral knell.

No answer came. But when at length
The storm had spent its furious strength,
And morning looked with timid eye
And rosy cheek across the sky,
Out from the rocky line of shore,
A score of wretched wreckers bore,
With voices toned like beasts of prey,
And eyes like starving wolves at bay.

They thought to find no sign of life,
After that elemental strife.
But Odin took them all aboard,
A sin-benighted, hungry horde;
He lightened half the cargo's weight,
And when, released from burdening freight,
The good ship rose and floated, then
He set the pumps at work again.
And like a weary, wounded swan,
With wings a-droop and beauty gone,
They kept her on her perilous way,
Slow and more slowly, up the bay,
On through the seething Gates of Hell,
Where baffled demons seemed to yell;

Around the light-house tower,
Across the uneasy harbor bar,
Till 'neath the placid evening star
They anchored safe, with home in sight;
And Odin's heart again grew light,
    With the conqueror's conscious power.
They bore the captain safe to land,
And with firm clasp on Odin's hand,
    He said, " I owe to you
The life which has come back again
Through terrible ordeal of pain;
And as God hears me, I will keep,
For your sake, till in death I sleep,
    One bond of friendship true."
How glad he was to leave again
His life upon the stormy main,
And with what joyous feet he trod
Again New England's soil and sod.

He marked the city's growth and change,
And the country looking cold and strange,
Following the tropic's regal sheen
And rich luxuriance of green.

But nothing charmed him like the snow.
So pure and cold, its wondrous glow
Allured him from the fireside warm,
To search amid the driving storm
For fancied pleasures, till he found
The far-off mountains closing round;
With all their wild, mysterious gloom,
They might have been a marble tomb.

He walked until the day grew dim,
And all the world was lost to him.
A faint, delicious languor crept
Across his brain. Almost he slept.
Almost his breathing seemed to cease;
He fell upon the mountain's fleece,
Its cool touch woke him; up he sprang,
And quick and sharp his rifle rang,
Waking the echoes far and clear,
To mock him as with answering cheer.

Again! again! and yet again!
And'peak and point and distant plain
Seemed filled with echoing battle strife,
And yet all sound or sign of life
In that white wilderness was gone!
He fell, and rose, and staggered on,
And fell again, at last, so low,
Beside the cliff, that all the snow,
O'erhanging, heavier than a cloud,
Fell too, and wrapped him like a shroud.
"And did he die that fearful night,
In spotless panoply of white?"
Not he! But if by searching hound
Or passing traveller he was found,
He knew not, till the morning broke,
And he from strangest dreaming woke,
To find a camp-fire burning near,
And loggers at their simple cheer.

When he came home, each thrilling nerve
And aching limb I thought would serve
To keep him with us many a day,
But business called him next away,

Far to the bright Pacific's shore,
With all its wealth of golden ore.
   *   *   *   *   *   *
Then his life grew the life of a pilgrim,
And change followed change very fast;
His letters were full of adventure,
Each seeming more strange than the last.

Sometimes he was up on the mountains,
Alone with his half-tamed mustang;
Then down in the warm, pleasant valleys,
That brighten that wide Western land.

And once he was lost on the desert,
Beyond e'en the cactus flowers bright,
Where no grateful shade intercepted
The sun, with its terrible light.

His horse had grown restless and lagging,
He heard the loose click of a shoe,
And so to remove it, dismounting,
The bridle his fingers slipped through.

And with one vicious snort, full of freedom,
The treacherous beast sped away,
While seven shining hours burned and brightened
Before the cool close of the day.

On he walked in the gleam and the glitter,
The sand yielded under his feet;
His brain seemed on fire, and his eyeballs
And throat were parched dry by the heat.

And still he toiled on, ever hoping
Some shelter or shade he might find,
And his horse still eluded his grasping,
And mockingly left him behind.

But at last, over-wearied and fainting,
He fell with his face to the sun;
He thought his good angel had left him,
That his life and its labor were done.

And while he lay there on the desert,
With reason and consciousness fled,
Some friend, far away in the Bay State,
Said suddenly, "Odin is dead."

In the borderland, dreamless and silent,
He wandered unconsciously, then,
But he was so strong that his spirit
Struggled back to his form once again.

And again his strange life of adventure
Flowed on, with its varying tide,
'Till it drifted him back to find anchor,
Once more, safe and fond, at my side.

* * * * * *

So having lived through flood and frost,
Sun-burned, snow-chilled, and tempest tost,
    Through suffering and pain,
I thought he would be satisfied
To linger here at Ingleside,
    Nor wish to roam again.

But oh, in one fair mystic hour
His heart thrilled with the unconscious power,

All other powers above.
The blind, blind god an arrow sent,
With most perverse and dire intent,
    And Odin fell in love.

He chose from out the world's gay throng
One star, whose radiance, pure and strong,
    Should gild life's darkest places;
One flower more sweet than others are,
And one face brighter than a star,
    Fairer than other faces.

He chose her for her gentle pride,
Her life's sweet, swerveless undertide
    Of purity and power;
To guide him on forevermore,
From stormy sea to sunny shore,
    Through every changeful hour.

And she? the wild ecstatic bliss
Of her first lover's first fond kiss
    Fell on her like a charm;
It came, her waiting lips to greet,
Blessing and benediction sweet,
    The echo of a psalm.

It told of cares and troubles o'er,
Peace for the present—hope in store,
    A future long and bright.
It hinted, happiest dream on earth,
Of home and children at the hearth,
    Light leading unto light.

And yet she strove with fluttering sigh
To put the proffered treasure by,
  He was so gay and young,
The very love he thought a boon
To-day, might prove a trouble soon;
  But closer kisses clung

About her brow, and lip, and cheek;
He smiled the faith he would not speak,
  And blessed her o'er and o'er.
The only truth their love could teach
Was this: that each belonged to each,
  Forever, evermore.

Alas! that those young hearts must find,
The bitter core beneath the rind
  That seemed so fair to view.
Alas! that pride of wealth or birth
Should crush the brightest hopes of earth,
  And make the truth less true.

  * * * * * *

Aunt Prudence paused, the radiant happy light
Was fading from her brown eyes, soft and bright,
When merry cousin Tom spoke next, as if
To exorcise the faintest hint or shade
Of sadness from our minds:

      "We all have heard,
That in some foreign country there are mines
Of salt, hid in great caverns underground,
And there the most unsightly stick or stone,
Or bit of jet-black coal or chalk-white bone,
Takes on itself a wondrous fairy dress
Of pure, clear crystals, beautified by salt.
Now, everybody knows that our Aunt Prue

Is nothing else but salt, all the way through.
Her heart, a cavern where she keeps her friends,
And by some mystic process all her own,
She crystallizes them, and beautifies
And so adorns them, that they would not know
Themselves; to make no mention of the chance
Of being recognized by friend or foe.
So with all grateful and most praiseful thanks,
For all the sweet and rhythmical device,
By which her pen and voice have charmed us here,
The last half-hour (and happier time ne'er sped),
Suppose we coax and flatter *cousin Luke*
To tell us all how Odin fell in love,
And how his suit was prospered."
       With one voice
Grandsire and Grandma, yes, and all the rest,
Laughed pleasantly at this ingenious mode
Of coaxing on the story-telling treat;
But after some discussion, pro and con,
Some faint demur, some talk of substitute,
Then, cousin Luke took up the broken thread
Of rhyming talk, a little awkwardly,
Perhaps, at first, but full of earnest zeal,
Of family preference and family spite,
 And, always, love for Odin.

III.

COUSIN LUKE'S STORY.

[ODIN'S LOVE EXPERIENCE.]

Our Odin was a handsome lad,
    With eyes of deepest blue,
And soft bright hair, like curls of flax,
    And sunlight shining through;
The dimples in his cheek and chin
    Gave him a baby air,
But by the firm grip of his hand,
    One knew him strong, as fair.

Judge Winthrop is a pompous man,
    Whose hair and eyes and skin
Are all one silky mousey gray;
    Deceitful, too, as sin.
He has one daughter, Helen,
    As proud as Lucifer;
I can't see where Aunt Prudence, here,
    Finds so much good in her.

I wish, for my part, she had been
    In Tophet, ere she set
Her wicked wits at work to catch
    Our Odin in her net.
You needn't shake your head at me,
    Aunt Prudence, for you know
She planned the whole thing out, for weeks.
    But there! We'll let that go.

She always rode the wildest colt
　　Upon her father's place.
One morning she was cantering off,
　　At her usual break-neck pace,
When a dusky gypsy baby
　　Lay before her in the road,
And just as she drew near to it,
　　The baby kicked, and crowed.

The horse, a vicious beast at best,
　　Reared high with sudden fright,
But Helen kept her seat, and would
　　Have brought him down all right,
Save that the treacherous bridle-rein
　　Snapped, like a slender thread;
The bit was loosed; and so, of course,
　　The beastie had his head.

Just then a strong young arm reached out,
　　All muscle, nerve, and brawn,
And Helen from her dangerous place
　　As quick as light was drawn;
While on his haunches crouched that horse
　　In sudden quietness.
Odin was giant-like in strength,
　　Child-like in gentleness.

He took the trembling figure in
　　His arms, and laid her there
With apple-blooms a-falling thick
　　As snow-flakes on her hair,
And when her two eyes opened, and
　　With tears of pain brimmed o'er,
The boy blushed—he had never been
　　So near a girl before.

He had to lift her up again,
    And bring her to Aunt Prue;
Of course she took and cuddled her,
    And knew just what to do;
Then Odin went and caught that colt,
    And rode him up the lane,
And told the Judge's stableman
    About the broken rein.

They sent a carriage down for her,
    She smiled, and rode away;
But she had stolen Odin's heart,
    That sunny summer day.
Aye, stolen! and I've cursed her
    'Till I could not breathe, for hate,
To think she dared to make herself
    An instrument of fate,

And drive our boy away from home—
    Oh, yes! I know, Aunt Prue,
She called him her preserver, and
    The Judge, he thought so too;
So he wrote a pompous letter, full
    Of thanks, and words of praise,
And wished the young man all success
    And length of future days.

"But he did not like to feel himself
    Indebted to a Pratt,
So if he'd accept a present—
    They'd call it square on that."

He wasn't like the other Pratts—
  Our Odin—or there'd been
A wider breach than ever
  Between the families, then.

He threw the letter in the fire,
  And laughed, and called it fudge,
And said "he'd really like to take
  A gift from that old Judge."
Then he met Helen every night,
  And rode with her, and walked,
And told her all his plans for life,
  And hoped, and dreamed, and talked.

Why! he had always been so shy,
  It didn't once occur
To us that *he* could fall in love,
  And least of all with *her*.
But she was born for flirting
  As a fish is made to swim,
And Odin, quite too earnest,
  To suspect a snare for him,

Called on that blamed old demagogue,
  And in his own frank way
Told him he loved his daughter
  Far more than words could say;
And asked his blessing and consent
  That she should be his wife,
When he had won a home for her,
  And was ready to start in life.

The old Judge didn't hear him out;
    He raved and swore like mad,
Enough to frighten anything,
    But a brave, true-hearted lad.
Said he, "Do you think my daughter
    Was born a natural fool,
That she should wait for any boy
    To starve his way through school?

"And you? Who are you, beggar?
    Who knows your name is Pratt?
What saves you from the alms-house fate
    Of any pauper brat?
Where were you born—if born at all?
    What was your mother's name?
What word or line have you to save
    Her memory from shame?"

Then all the slow, cool blood rushed up
    Through Odin's veins, like fire,
And burned his cheek, and lit his eye
    With fierce and sudden ire.
His clear-toned voice rang strangely out
    With a burst of foreign speech,
His two hands seemed to clench themselves
    For something out of reach,

And fell so near the Judge's head,
    It made him shrink away,
As though from some young lion who
    Would claim him for its prey.

*   *   *   *   *   *

"I never really knew what happened next,"
Said cousin Luke, "but Grandma knows it all."
"Yes, children," Grandma's voice crept softly in,
"Odin came home, looking as he had seen
A dozen ghosts, or something stranger still;
And leaning his bright head on his two hands,
Asked, 'Grandma, who am I ? oh, tell me, now,
Or, I am certain, I shall die, shall *die.*'
I told him—what you all have heard before—
About his coming to us, and I said,
'I have no doubt that Thomas and his wife
Were on that vessel, coming home to us.
But those strange countries always are at war,
And they were lost, and only you were left.'
Then father took from some place in his desk
The two old letters that for twenty years
Had lain there, catching dust and fading out;
And Odin glanced them o'er with wistful eyes,
Then folded them, and said, 'Give them to me;
They are the book of fate, and I must read.'
Next morn he went away—to Boston first,
And then to Washington, and after that
(His letter said) to Norway. So we wait,
And 'tis my daily hope and nightly prayer
That he will yet come home with tidings true
About my boy, my Thomas.
                    "None can know,
Save those whose hearts have ached from such a cause,
How terrible is waiting and suspense."

A silence fell upon the gathered group.
Then dear Aunt Margaret raised her voice a bit,
Just making it scarce louder, but more clear,
And said, "Do you remember, Father, when,

One winter, we were living in New York,
And you and mother came to visit us?"
"Why, surely, child, I never shall forget,"
Said Grandsire, glowing with grave interest;
"My friend, the General, lived on the next block.
His daughter Anna since has made a book—
'Hand-book of English Literature,' I think
They call it—and it brings its winsome share
Of fame to the young writer. It was there
I saw the Quaker poet, Whittier;
He came with his friend Channing, for a day.
And, though I must have been threescore years old,
And nearly twoscore a professor strict,
I never seemed to know or think before
About the Love of God. The kindly care
Which the All Father never ceasing keeps,
Through all His means, and over all His works,
It was a blessed thing to hear those men,
Cultured and kindly, talk of the divine
And universal love that rules the world.
There, too, came Lucy Hooper, Henry Clay,
And Frederika Bremer, noble souls,
Each trained in different schools of worldly life,
But every one complete in their own way.
How few of them are living now," he said,
And breathed a sigh; then presently resumed:
"The General was a strong and steadfast man,
He swore by Chalmers with such earnest faith,
As I by Calvin; but, I think we both
Grew liberal while listening to the words
Of gentle Channing."
      Grandsire paused and mused;
And Uncle 'Liab was the first to break
The silent charm.

"Father! you never knew
How near your wakened love for Channing came
To making trouble in the family?"
"To making trouble! How?" and Grandsire's face
Put on a look of wonder, queer to see.
"Well! you and mother know that Parson Flint
Had always some strange tenets in his creed,
About fore-ordination, and the like;
Something of close communion, too; but that
I never cared so much about. At first
I did not know that Betsey meant to keep
Those most objectionable forms of faith;
And when I found she did, I used to sneer,
Sometimes, about them; and it angered her.
And so we went from bad to something worse,
'Till, finally, the Unitarians
Started their meetings in the old Town Hall.
Channing was coming there to preach for them!
And then I spoke of going. Well; it seemed
As though the vials of eternal wrath
Were being poured through Betsey's tongue on me;
'Twas only scold, scold, scold, from morn 'till night;
Nothing I did was right or could be right.
But, spite of all she said, and I said too,
Spite of her scolding, and me answering back,
When that bright, sunny Sunday morning came
I walked with Betsey to the Baptist church,
And left her there, and went with surly steps
Across the common, to the old Town Hall,
And took a seat, and listened.
                    In the desk
There stood a pale-browed, quiet, delicate man,
With, even then, a slight, sharp, hacking cough;
But oh, his eyes were brighter than two stars;

And the deep, thrilling sweetness of his voice,
Possessed me like the haunting of a dream,
For many days. Then how I tried to talk
With Betsey, of the beautiful new truths
That seemed to be just dawning on my soul.
But 'twas no use; she only scolded more;
And I more angry and impatient grew.
She twitted me of every scaly thing
I ever said or done. While I, you know,
Was never very ready with my tongue;
But that was no excuse for us at all.
At last, I swore, by all most sacred things,
I wouldn't bear with her another day.
I'd go and find a lawyer, and we'd have
The farm divided, and I'd go away."
"Oh, child! my boy!" here Grandma's voice broke in,
"You wronged yourself in thinking to obtain
Comfort or peace from human justice then;
You should have gone straight to the throne of grace."
"Mother," said Uncle 'Liab, with a smile,
"The throne of grace seemed too far off just then,
And human justice was a very near
And very spiteful thing; easy to reach.
At any rate I carried out my threat—
I went to see a lawyer, and says I—.

IV.

UNCLE 'LIAB'S STORY.

[BETSEY AND I ARE OUT.]

Draw up the papers, lawyer,
    And make 'em good and stout,
For things at home are crosswise,
    And wife and I are out.
You ask me "What's the matter?"
    I vow it's hard to tell;
Our married life for so far
    Has passed by tol'rable well;

I have no other woman,
    She has no other man,
Only we've lived together
    As long as we think we can.
So I have talked with Betsey,
    And Betsey has talked with me,
And we have agreed together
    That we can't never agree.

Not that we've catched each other
    In any terrible crime,
But trouble has been a brewin'
    Between us for quite a time.
The first thing very essential
    Whereon we disagreed,
Was something concernin' Heaven—
    A difference in our creed.

We argued the thing at breakfast,
    We argued the thing at tea,
And the more we argued the question
    The more we didn't agree;
And the next that I remember
    Was, when we lost a cow—
The critter had kicked the bucket,
    The question was only how.

I held my own opinion,
    And Betsey another had,
And as we talked about it
    We both of us grew mad.
And the next was when I called her
    A Pusseyite, half for a joke,
And full for a week thereafter
    No word to me she spoke.

And then I scolded sharply
    When she broke a china bowl;
And she said I was mean and stingy,
    And hadn't any soul;
And so that bowl kep' pourin'
    Dissensions in our cup,
And so that blamed cow critter
    Was always a-comin' up.

And so the Heaven we argued
    No nearer to us came,
But it gave us a taste of something
    With a hotter-sounding name.
And so the trouble gathered
    All in the self-same way—
Always something to argue,
    And something sharp to say.

'Till down on us come the neighbors,
  A couple o' dozen strong,
And lent their kindest sarvice,
  To help the thing along;
And there have been days together,
  And many a weary week,
We were both of us proud and spunky,
  And both too cross to speak.

And I have been thinkin' and thinkin',
  For the whole of the summer and fall,
If I can't live kind with a woman,
  I wont live with her at all.
So what is hers shall be hers,
  And what is mine be mine;
You just make out the agreement
  And I'll take it to her to sign.

Now, then! Put down on the paper,
  The very first paragraph,
That of all the farm and live stock,
  Betsey shall have her half;
For she has helped to earn it,
  Through many a weary day,
And it's nothing more than justice
  She has her honest pay.

Give her the house and homestead;
  A man can thrive and roam,
But women are skeery critters
  Unless they have a home.
And I have always determined,
  And never failed to say,
That Betsey should have a home of her own
  If I was taken away.

Then there's a little hard money
    Laid by for a rainy day;
Just a few hundred dollars,
    That's drawing tol'rable pay,
Safe in the hands of good men,
    And easy to come at;
Put in another clause there,
    And give her half of that.

Yes, I see you smile, sir,
    At my giving her so much;
You say divorce is cheap, sir,
    But I take no stock in such;
True and fair I married her,
    When she was blithe and gay,
And she sha'n't have cause to blame me,
    Now I am going away.

Once, when I was young as you,
    And not so smart, perhaps,
For me she mittened a lawyer,
    And several other chaps;
And all of them was flustered
    And mightily taken down,
And I for a time was counted
    The luckiest man in town.

And after we were married,
    Oh, she was happy and strong;
It made my heart feel lighter
    To hear her merry song.
She nursed me through a fever
    When the doctors said I'd die;
For seven nights hand-running
    She never shut her eye.

And if ever a house was tidy,
    And ever a kitchen clean,
Her house and kitchen were tidy
    As any I've ever seen.
So I don't complain of Betsey
    For anything she's done,
It's only for the thorning
    Of her everlasting tongue.

And I don't blame it all on Betsey,
    I'm willin' to take my share,
Only her constant scolding
    Is more than I can bear.
So make out the papers, lawyer,
    And I'll go home to-night
And read the agreement to her,
    And see if it's all right.

And then I'll sell in the morning
    To a trading man I know,
And I'll kiss our little Bessie
    And out in the world I'll go.
You see that's one great reason
    I couldn't divorce my wife,
'Twould be a disgrace to Bessie
    For all the rest of her life.

And one thing put in the paper,
    That first to me didn't occur—
That, when I die, I want some one
    To take me back to her,
And lay me under the maples
    I planted so long ago,
When Betsey and I was happy,
    Before we quarrelled so.

And when she dies, it's my wish
    That she should be lain by me ;
And, lying together in silence,
    Perhaps we'll learn to agree :
And when we meet in Heaven,
    I wouldn't think it queer
If we loved each other better
    For having quarrelled here.

    *   *   *   *   *   *

"That was a strange idea of yours, I think,"
Said Grandsire, gravely ; "Failing to agree
On earth could scarcely be supposed to be
A passport for much harmony in Heaven."
"And, too," said cousin John, respectfully,
"Begging your pardon, sir, for what may seem
Presumption on my part, I think divorce
Should never be considered a disgrace;
It only means : We two thought we could live
In peace and harmony for all our lives ;
We tried and failed ; we therefore wish henceforth
To go our separate ways on life's highway,
Free from all bond or ban."
                            Then Grandma said :
"Children, we will not here and now discuss
A question of such serious import."
    And Grandsire, turning to Aunt Betsey, asked,
"But, daughter, had you no wise word to say,
When things had taken such a serious turn?"
Aunt Betsey's face flushed brightly as she said,
"Oh, father, I am ashamed that you should know
Our folly and our weakness and our sin ;
Let's drop the unpleasant subject, if you please."
"And have a song ; the theme is growing sad
And solemn as a church," cried cousin Tom ;

"Here, take this fragment; I have scribbled it
While Uncle 'Liab talked." And so they sang—

THE FIRST QUARREL.

1.

The church-bells were ringing,
The wild birds were singing,
When 'Liab and I started out from our door,
    With Bessie between us,
    Her dimpled hands swinging,
Her laugh was so light that it would bubble o'er.

2.

Three weeks I'd been waiting,
'Twixt hoping and hating,
For this Sunday morning; and now it had come;
    I'd coaxed him and petted,
    And scolded and fretted,
And hoped the new preacher might be stricken dumb.

3.

But slow and more slowly,
The day seemed so holy,
In silence we walked, till we reached the church-door;
    "I'm going to hear Channing,"
    Said 'Liab's voice, lowly,
"I'll call for you here when the service is o'er."

4.

Then love's eyes grew glassy,
My wedding-ring brassy;

A thousand small demons laughed out with a cry,
    And all through the singing
      Their voices were ringing,
"You've quarrelled"—I knew they meant 'Liab and I.
   *   *   *   *   *   *
But Grandma could not let the matter rest,
For she was grieved and puzzled; so she said:
"Can it be, Betsey, that a boy of mine
Could be so rash and foolish as to treat
His own home troubles in that public way?"
Aunt Betsey blushed again, and put her hair
Back, with a weary gesture from her brows,
Her thin gray hair, that once was brown and bright.
"I do not like to talk of it," she said;
But all their questioning eyes decided her,
And hesitating shyly, she began—

V.

AUNT BETSEY'S STORY.

[How Husband and I Made Up.]

Yes! 'Liab brought home from the lawyer's
    That paper for me to sign,
Saying, what was his should *be* his,
    And what was mine be mine.
For 'Liab and I had quarrel'd
    So many times, you see,
That at last we agreed together
    We couldn't never agree.

So I read the paper over,
    Each separate paragraph,
And found, that of all our property
    He'd given me the better half;
For he gave me the house and homestead,
    And kept the Wolf Rock hill,
He gave me the colt Saladin,
    And kept the lame horse, Bill.

He gave me the brindled heifer,
    (The line-back cow was dead,)
But he gave me the sheep and oxen,
    And kept the steers, instead;
I was mad because he favored me,
    And made it show so plain,
And I 'spose if he hadn't done so much,
    I should only been mad again;

But looking along the paper,
    The next thing that I read,
Was, "Lay us under the maples
    Together, when we're dead."
Then I knew the one choice left me,
    Was a flood of tears or tongue;
So I told him, "I wouldn't sign the thing
    To save him from bein' hung.

"In his mean old farm and live-stock,
    I scorned any part or share;
I was goin' home to my mother,
    And 'twas none of his business! There."
Then straight in my face looked 'Liab,
    Till I turned my head away;
And he walked out through the kitchen,
    Not another word to say;

I heard his steps fall heavy,
    But I didn't see him go;
The maples were blushing scarlet
    He planted so long ago.
And under them played our Bessie,
    Child of our happy years,
I heard her calling "Papa,"
    And then came a rush of tears;

But before I could reach the door-way
    Click went the garden gate,
And to all my sorrowful feelings
    It seemed to say—"too late."
Then Bessie came in from her playing,
    A tear on each round red cheek;
And asked, "Where's Papa going?
    He kissed me, but did not speak."

Then up in my arms I caught her,
  And murmured and sobbed her name,
Bewailing that ever my darling
  Was born to such woe and shame.
Forgetting all thought of doctrine,
  Or halving of stock and store,
I wanted my baby's father
  Safe in my heart once more.

But 'Liab was gone! the sunshine
  Lay golden along the lane,
I strained my eyes with watching,
  But he didn't turn back again;
And thinkin' the whole thing over,
  I blamed him bitter and strong;
I was glad he had held his tongue once,
  He always was in the wrong.

I thought he'd be back that evening,
  But the sleepless night dragged on,
And still no whisper told me
  What way had my husband gone.
'Twas Thursday when he left me,
  At last came Saturday night;
How slowly I swept the dooryard
  And set the old house to rights.

Then I cuddled and rocked my Bessie,
  While she said, "Now I lay me," sweet,
Till her eyes drooped, and I laid her
  In her old crib, fast asleep.
But oh! how I did miss 'Liab—
  I'd ha' given half my life
To hear his dear voice saying,
  "Where are you, Betsey, wife?"

But there was a prayer-meeting gathered
    That night by Deacon Munroe,
I thought I'd stay at home first,
    And then I concluded to go;
For the neighbors know'd we'd quarrelled,
    And, as 'Liab always said,
They'd lent their kindest sarvice
    For to help the thing ahead.

But that night they turned up their noses,
    With a smile that was more a sneer,
And said, "Where's Mr. Pratt, pray?
    Why isn't he with you here?"
I was mad as a pestered hornet,
    Though I tried to be proud and cool,
But I blamed them all for hypocrites,
    And hated myself for a fool!

So, when I could bear it no longer,
    And the Deacon was praying still,
I slipped out and hurried homeward,
    Alone, by the Wolf Rock hill;
Silent I entered the kitchen,
    And silently crossed the floor;
But my heart stood still a minute,
    As I opened the bedroom door.

For there was my dear old 'Liab
    A kneeling by Bessie's bed;
And some tears shone on the pillow
    That Bessie never had shed.
One look! and the very next minute
    I was kneeling beside him there;
And more tears fell on the pillow,
    And some on our darling's hair.

Well! under the old rose blankets,
    That were new on our wedding-day,
And under the patchwork coverlet,
    We found it was better to lay,
Than under the thrifty maples
    (They've doubled in size since then),
And if the Recordin' Angel
    Came down with his book and pen

That night, I know the last record
    He took to his higher sphere
Was, "Betsey, wife, are you sorry?"
    "Husband, I'm glad you're here."
Next morning we burned the paper
    We both had forgotten to sign.
I didn't ask his forgiveness,
    And he didn't beg for mine.

But we both pretty much concluded,
    Without any words to tell,
That what was mine was his'n,
    And his'n was mine as well.
And when we meet in Heaven,
    I wouldn't think it queer,
If we loved each other better
    For bein' patient here.

*   *   *   *   *   *

I saw the tears shining in Grandma's eyes;
But as Aunt Betsey finished with a smile,
Her hand slid under Uncle 'Liab's palm,
And rested there. Then Uncle Luke looked up;
A droll and quizzical smile was on his face,
And without form or prelude he began.

VI.

UNCLE LUKE'S STORY.

[Going to Channing's Meeting.]

Bein' we're at confession,
    And 'Liab's had his say,
And Betsey's told her story
    In her own forgivin' way.
Though you mayn't have quite suspected
    The nater of the fuss,
Yet goin' to Channing's meeting
    Came near upsetting *us*.

I, too, heard father talkin'
    About the light and love
That raised this wondrous preacher
    All meaner souls above.
And I said, I meant to hear him;
    But Priscilla, she said, "Nay;
From the teachin's of our fathers
    It wouldn't do to stray."

I arger'd personal freedom,
    Especially for a man,
And said we couldn't grow a bit
    On any other plan.
So evenin' after evenin'
    I'd stop, awhile, to hear
Some earnest Unitarian
    Discuss their doctrines queer.

I knew it fretted Prissie,
　　I see it in her eye;
And if I spoke about it,
　　She was allers sure to cry.
But when the famous Channing,
　　With his words of love for all,
Was comin' for one Sunday
　　To preach in the old Town Hall,

Sez I, "It's no use talkin';
　　I've nothin' more to say;
But I'll go to that there meetin',
　　If I die for't on the way."
Well! so I went, next Sunday,
　　Just as I vowed I would;
The words were mild and gentle,
　　I hope they done me good.

But while I listened, steady,
　　A voice seemed whispering through,
"There's Prissie up to the Baptists
　　A thinkin' hard of you."
After the meetin' was over,
　　They didn't much mind me,
But I heard more'n one say softly,
　　"*There's* Deacon 'Liab—*see!*"

I know'ed he'd get a scoldin'
　　When he got home from church,
Which I rather guessed he dreaded
　　As a school-boy dreads the birch.
Though I hadn't much to brag on,
　　For all to myself I said,
I'd rather a woman would scold me,
　　Than cry the eyes out of her head.

So home I went, with a feelin'
    As though I'd done su'thin' wrong,
And would like to cuss somebody,
    If somebody 'd come along.
And, just as I expected,
    Priscilla was hidin' away,
A crying about my futur',
    As she did for many a day;

Till it made me mad as the mischief
    Only to see her cry.
I tried first to pacify her,
    And fin'ly I sez, sez I:
"I ain't a-going to stan' it,
    Now; I tell you what it is,
I've borne with these proceedin's
    Till my dander's fairly riz.

"I've tried to live in quiet,
    As becomes a man and wife,
But I'll pull in single harness
    For the rest o' my nateral life
Afore I'll bear this frettin'
    And yowlin' night an' day,
That don't do you no sort o' good,
    And wears my life away.

"I am going to our parson,
    To tell him where I've been,
And if I hev committed
    The unpardonable sin,
I'll leave the place forever,
    And not be stayin' here,
To drag you to perdition,
    Or break your heart with fear."

So off in a huff I started,
    But scarcely reached the gate,
When I met my friend, Squire Osborne,
    With Channing. I didn't wait
To stand on ceremony,
    But inimejitly asked 'em in.
We talked of the crops and the weather,
    And then of original sin;

Of the old Town Hall, and the taxes,
    Of the efficacy of prayer,
And finally of the meeting
    Last Sunday—and who was there.
Then the Squire went off to the village,
    And Channing he staid with me;
'Twas then I told him my troubles,
    And what they was like to be.

He said 'twas my selfish temper
    Was shadowin' all my life,
That I must respect the conscience
    And principles of my wife,
As her individual privilege,
    And not as a cause for strife.
Then, to make it sound religious,
    He said such trials were given
To teach us strength and patience,
    And lead us up to Heaven.

He said, her weak complainin',
    Was a cross that I must bear;
And if I bore it bravely,
    I'd be rewarded there.

It comforted me to hear him
    Talking that kind of a way;
I made up my mind I'd scolded
    Too much, and so from that day,

I'd be sort o' kind to Prissie,
    And just let her cry it out,
And not be continually asking
    What she was cryin' about.
So I walked down town with Channing,
    Shook hands, and said, good-by;
Went home, and wife was a lookin'
    As though she'd forgot how to cry.

I spoke kind o' pleasant to her,
    She smiled, and I went along;
And soon in the yard I heard her
    Humming a sweet old song.
That night 'twas the same, and next day,
    With not a tear to be seen;
Never a home was brighter,
    Or sunshine more serene;
'Till at last I begun to wonder
    Whatever it all could mean.

I'd talk, and Priscilla would answer—
    Sober, sometimes, it's true,
And her lip would sorter quiver,
    And her eyes shine brighter, too.
But never a fretful word came,
    And never a tear-drop fell.
Bimeby I thought of the story
    That Deacon Munroe used to tell,

About his wife, and the crooked wood.
    You don't remember it? No?
Well, I dunno as I can tell it,
    But I b'lieve 'twas somehow *so:*
The Deacon was talkin' with 'Liab
    'Bout the minister's meetin' near,
And 'Liab said he was anxious
    To know how many 'd be here,

So 's he could talk with Betsey
    'Bout askin' of 'em home.
The Deacon said, 'twan't easy
    To tell how many 'd come.
" But surely in a household
    So large and well-to-do,
A few guests more, I'm thinkin',
    Can't make much odds to you."

" No," 'Liab answered slowly,
    As though 'twas wrong he told,
" But anything unexpected
    Is sure to make wife scold."
" Sho ! " said the Deacon gravely,
    As though he'd heard some news ;
" But my wife never scolds me,
    So I have no excuse."

" Never ? " sez 'Liab, questioning ;
    " Never a frown on her brow ? "
" Never ! " the Deacon answered,
    " I expect she don't know how.
She allers sez what ain't right
    Will be right, by and by.
And if we want a thing done,
    We've only jest to try.

"Till sometimes, she's so quiet
    It agravates me wuss
Than any sort o' scoldin'
    Or any amount o' fuss."
"Well! neow, I think," says 'Liab,
    "If you hanker arter a scold,
I kin tell you how to git one;
    I know the way, of old.

"Jest take her a load o' crooked wood,
    An' if she don't fret at that,
Why, the day o' the minister's meetin'
    I'll give you a Sunday hat."
So the Deacon went to his wood lot
    Himself, and cut a load
Of the gnarliest, meanest, crooked stuff,
    I swan, that ever growed.

An' he took it home, an' waited,
    An' watched, day after day,
Clean down to one last armful,
    To hear what she would say.
An' when she found 'twas all gone,
    Sez she, "I wish, my dear,
I had another load o' wood
    Like the last you brought me here.

"The sticks were kinder curvin,
    And sorter seemed to slide
And fit round the pots an' kittles
    The best I ever tried."
The Deacon didn't answer
    Aloud, but all to himself,
Sez he, "Old hat! hereafter
    Your place is on the shelf."

Well! So, as I was sayin',
  I thought o' that load o' wood,
And wondered if some apple-tree brush
  Wouldn't be quite as good,
For trying a woman's patience;
  For everybody knows
That women do hate apple-tree brush
  The wust of all wood that grows.

So out I went to the orchard,
  And trimmed, and trimmed those trees,
And drove home a load to the door-yard,
  As solemn as ever you please.
Priscilla, she saw it a coming,
  And wondering, looked at me;
Then she burst out laughin' as merry
  As a mocking-bird on a tree.

Sez she, "There's nothin' like brush, Luke,
  On wash-days, for b'ilin' the clothes;
And as for my cryin' about it,
  Now would I, do you suppose?"
That made me feel sort 'er sheepish;
  I expect I looked so, too;
But sez I, "Now, Prissie, tell me!
  What has come over you?

I never find you frettin';
  You don't appear to cry;
It must be *you* that's changed so,
  I'm sure it can't be I."
Sez she, "I heerd that lesson
  By your good friend, Channing, given.
I sha'n't be made a scape-goat
  For carryin' *you* to Heaven."

So then we talked it over;
   An' if she cried a bit
Her face was hid on my shoulder,
   So I didn't notice it;
But the boys had a jolly bonfire
   Of apple-tree brush that night,
And you might have seen a farmer
   Kissing his wife by its light.

*   *   *   *   *   *

While all the others laughed, Grandma looked sad,
And said, "My boys, I really am afraid
You do not do as I have always taught,
And make your troubles subjects of home prayer."
   The brothers looked askance, but answered not.
For a loud shout came ringing on the air,
And a gay voice called out, "Shure it's meself
As towld ye spalpeens I wad let ye know
Whin I was ready to shet up the barn.
Turn out if so be you would like to see
The beasties once ag'in." Then Cousin Tom,
And Uncle Christopher, and Uncle King
All hastened barnward with the troop of boys,
And Pat, the hostler, whistling as they went.
But as Tom left the room, grave Cousin John
Looked up and said: "There goes the truest soul
That ever kept a living flame of faith,
And love for all mankind, through every ill.
You laugh at his light jests and merry words,
But reck not of the depth of kindly thought,
Self-abnegation, and true courtesy
That underlie them all.

                           He too has wrought,
And toiled, and suffered. Striven long and well,

And just when he had thought to stand upon
The very brink of triumph, sorrow came.
We were together long ago at school,
And somewhat later, when I studied law
And he plunged into medicine ; I knew
He had some philanthropic hopes and plans ;
But, when we went to California,
The golden glitter tempted him. He thrust
Aside, in one ambitious, reckless hour,
His loved profession and the hopes he held,
And launched one more frail barque upon the tide
  Of speculation. Everything he touched
Seemed to have felt the old King Midas' power,
  And turned to gold.
                  I knew he was engaged
To Mercy Lincoln. Some of you have seen
Her fair child-face, as lovely as a dream ;
You know her father was a strange old man ;
A miser and a monomaniac.
He seemed to think that every one he met
Was striving to obtain the hoarded wealth
That he had saved for Mercy.
                      Tom soon learned
The only passport to the old man's heart
Was by a golden key. He knew before,
That Mercy never would be coaxed to wed
Without his blessing. So by day and night
He strove for money—thus to win his bride,
Poor Tom ! I found a bit of rhyme one day
That Nettie wrote of him : I'll read it now
And it shall serve as ' story ' told by me."

VII.

COUSIN JOHN'S STORY.

[IN CALIFORNIA.]

HE climbed the wild heights of ambition and pride,
Wealth poured at his feet her bewildering tide,
Friends gathered about him to court and caress
(Friends always appreciate certain success).
And fairer than old ruined temple or tower
His home rose in beauty and light hour by hour,
His home, where full soon, as he dreamed, would be heard
The musical voice of his own precious bird.
Their home ! where all beautiful ideals were ;
He had fashioned, and furnished, and decked it for her.
He would go soon to bring her. When—never a word
Of warning or trouble or doubt had he heard,
No breath in the air, and no cloud in the sky,
Had hinted what awful bereavement was nigh.
But suddenly came, like a messenger dread,
A letter that told him his darling was dead.
Dead ! Dead ! And he loved her, aye, worshipped her so !
Dead ! How his heart sickened and reeled 'neath the blow.
How all hope's gay sunshine paled strangely and fled,
As he thought of his darling, his precious love, dead !
No kiss on her cold lips, no whispered farewell,
No murmur of faith or endearment to tell
To his agonized heart, that she took o'er the river
One memory of him that would linger forever.

Ah! what to him, now, was the pretty home nest
With every adornment that Love could suggest?
The cup that had almost been raised to his lips
Dashed suddenly down in that awful eclipse.
'Twas hard to relinquish that beautiful dream;
Cold, dark, and uncertain the future must seem,
As he took up again the dropped shuttle of fate,
And hopelessly wove on his life-web—to wait.

But soon to his soul-life, with comforting power
The angel of Faith brought a beautiful dower;
He thought of the hopes that had lighted *her* way
Down through the dark valley, where, day after day,
The angels talked with her, and walked by her side,
And brought her sweet peace, *his* dear love, but *death's* bride.
And then, as his life-path grew harder to climb,
As he dreamed more and more of her presence divine,
She drew nearer to him in spirit and thought;
He fancied she cared for the labor he wrought.

That, when he had turned from the glare of the day,
The gold and the glitter, the fret and the fray,
She lingered beside him forever the same;
So his darling an angel of mercy became.
Then his life was no more filled with sorrow and pain;
The dreams of his boyhood came back once again.

He left the excitement, the turmoil, the strife,
And bravely returned to his worthier life;
Wherever was darkness, or danger, or death,
Contagion, or trouble, or fever's hot breath,
There stood the physician, the brother, the friend,
Unflinching and steadfast, and true to the end.

If he falls, he will fall with his face to the light,
For Mercy is with him—his guardian bright.

* * * * * *

When Cousin John stopped talking, and a hush
Of sympathy and sorrow fell upon
The earnest listeners, Captain Philip Brown
Said gently, speaking to his fair-haired wife :
" Emily, was it for him you wrote the song
I often hear you trilling to yourself,
About the roses, and the work to do?"
Emily smiled, and nodded. " Sing it, please,"
Pleaded the cousins; and so Emily sang—

My Darling.

Under the roses and myrtles bright,
Under the lilies so daintily white,
Under the blue forget-me-nots true,
  My beautiful darling is sleeping.
Hushed is the voice that I loved to hear,
Closed are the brown eyes, soft and clear,
    Heart-beat and breath
    Are frozen in death;
Lonely and sad I am weeping.

Years have passed since they laid her there,
Years of trouble, and grief, and care,
Yet over the space gleams an angel face,
  Guiding and blessing me ever.
Though her voice is hushed to mine outward ear,
In spirit its echoing tones I hear.
    I know she will wait
    By the golden gate
To meet me where death cannot sever.

Therefore I pause not for dreaming or dread;
The sad call for comfort, the hungry for bread;
Why should I fear, when angels are near,
    Or shrink from the Summer-land portal?
The way is long, but the goal is bright,
Dawn will follow the darkest night,
    And I know *she* will come
      To welcome me home,
My darling, for love is immortal.

    *   *   *   *   *   *

The song was scarce done echoing when there came
A burst of merry laughter, and the boys
Came rushing in, and gathered round the fire.
And Pat, the hostler, and a friend of his
Came with them; Pat explaining that he heard
That they were telling stories hereabouts,
And his old friend was such a master hand
To be a-telling shtories—never yet
He'd heerd of one too big for him to tell;
Or yet to take and swallow.
                      Pat's bright eyes
Were twinkling full of drollery; but his face
Was calm and solemn.
                    Then his friend drew back
Within the shadow, tipped his battered hat,
And swinging his shillalah, 'gan to talk:

"Shure it's no shtory I wud till ye now,
But just a dhrame my frind Pat tells me he
Enjoyed one summer even."
                Thus says Pat:

VIII.

UNCLE KING'S STORY.

[Pat's Dream of Heaven.]

I DHRAMED I wint to Hiven one night,
    And knocked at the big white gate,
And the good Saint Pater opened it,
    But he towld me I'd have to wait
While he looked for me name in the howly book;
    And when he had found it there,
He bad me come in, though he towld me plain
    That me comin' that way was rare.

Well, I shtopped a bit to chat wid him,
    And I axed, "Could I look around?"
He said, "Oh yis! as you've once got in,
    Yer frae to the whole of the ground—
Frae to walk by the River of Life,
    To resht in the Mansions of Light,
To stand in the Temple not made by hands,
    Wid the Sunburst of Glory bright."

I saw the Martyrs of owlden times,
    The saints and the angels fair,
And millions and millions of young spalpeens
    All playin' t'gither there;
And Mary the Mother, wid love in her eyes,
    Looked down on each little child,
And the blissed tacher was tachin' them,
    So gintle and undefiled.

I saw the Apostles a mending their nets,
  And I axed, "What need of thim now?"
Then a howly light shone round about
  Each lowly Apostle's brow,
As they said: "Our nets must nades be shtrong
  For to lift men's sowls away
From the darkness and doubt they're clingin' in,
  To the light of the perfect day."

But away in a corner I heard a noise;
  I thought 'twas a bit of a row,
So I loosed my Shillalah—"Be gorra," sez I,
  "If it's fightin', I'll jist show 'em how."
But when I drew nearer I heard them shpake,
  And Paul was a-tellin' aloud
A shtory of Joseph the Carpenter,
  To a listening bit of a crowd.

Now, Joseph, it sames, was a good-natured sowl,
  And what he was towld he belaved;
And many's the frind, on his recommind,
  By Pater had been resaved.
But Pater at last found this wouldn't do,
  So he towld to the Carpenter Joe,
That no more frinds on his recommind
  Inside of the gates should go.

Then what does Joseph the Carpenter do,
  But, bein' so deft at his thrade,
He wint to work wid hammer and plane,
  And a long shtrong ladder he made;
And thrustin' it out of a windy high,
  Afore they guessed what he's about,
He was snakin' his frinds by the dozens in;
  And that was what caused the rout.

For Paul the pr'acher, the earnest heart,
    Had found what was goin' on,
And he wus a-tellin' the shtory shtrange
    To Mathew and Mark and John;
And Pater the doorkaper left his place,
    And dhrew near and listened too,
Till he waxed very wroth, "Now, Joseph," sez he,
    "We've had too much throuble with you.

Let me hear no more of these wicked pranks,
    Or we'll howld a council of war,
And see if there's no way of makin' you
    Abide by the common Law.
Why! we'll have you turned out as our inemy
    The Dhragon was, long ago,
And thin you must wandher in fear and doubt
    For a thousand years, you know."

Thin Joseph the Carpenter sadly said:
    "Is it turnin' me out, you mane?
Shure I'll go at wunst if you think it's best,
    And niver a word I'll complain.
But a man has a right to his family, Paul,"
    Here he winked his eye, and shmiled,
"And 'twould break up your whole institution, sure,
    If I take my wife and child."

Then all the Apostles took up their nets,
    And silently walked away;
And Pater moved off, a scratchin' his head
    Wid the end of the golden kay;
And Joseph the Carpenter whistled a tune,
    I thought 'twas a bit of a joke,
But I feared to laugh, so I made up my mind
    'Twas all a dhrame, and I woke.

    *   *   *   *   *   *

A roar of laughter shook the farm-house roof
That might have scared the owls.
                    Pat's friend threw off
His ragged jacket and his battered hat;
Pat caught them quick, and with a parting grin
Hurried away, while straight before us stood—
Why! Uncle King. His bright eyes brimming o'er
With merriment he did not try to hide,
Half at the wicked story he had told,
And half at the strange wonder he beheld
On every face!
                    "I knew how it would be,"
He said, and rubbed his hands with hearty glee.
"I knew you'd keep on telling stories here,
And I should have no peace 'till I would add
My quota to the general merriment;
So I forestalled the possible invite
And won my parents' disapproval too,
I sadly fear!—oh! mother mine, forgive
The careless jest, and I will promise now
To be a better boy henceforth!" And down
He bent his graceful form and grand great head
Whereon the frosts of threescore years lay white;
And grandma smiled, and blessed him, and forgave.

"Now pass along the stories! Whose turn next?"
Called Cousin Tom, and "Yours! Why, yours, of course,"
Came quick for answer; but he said, "No! No!"
"I have been gone so long, I want to hear
More of the village news. I heard the bells
From Woodend Parish ringing long ere night.
Grandsire, do you know what the cause could be?
Your home is thereabouts now, as of old."
    And then for answer came:

IX.

DEACON MUNROE'S STORY.

[CHURCH DISCIPLINE.]

YES, surely the bells in the steeple
    Were ringing; I thought you knew why.
No? Well, then, I'll tell you, though mostly
    It's whispered about on the sly;
Some six weeks ago, a church meeting
    Was held, for—nobody knew what;
But we went, and the Parson was present,
    And I don't know who, or who not.

Some twenty odd members, I calc'late,
    Which mostly was wimmin, of course;
But I don't mean to say aught agin 'em,
    I've seen many gatherings look worse.
And, in the front row sat the deacons,
    The eldest was old Deacon Pryor,
A man countin' fourscore and seven,
    And ginerally full of his ire!

Beside him, his wife, aged fourscore,
    A kind-hearted, motherly soul;
And next to her, young Deacon Hartley,
    A good Christian man, on the whole!
Miss Parsons, a spinster of fifty,
    And long ago laid on the shelf,
Had wedged herself next, and beside her
    Was Deacon Munroe. That's myself.

The meeting was soon called to order,
  The parson looked glum as a text;—
We silently stared at each other,
  And every one wondered, "What next?"
When straightway uprose Deacon Hartley,
  His voice seemed to tremble with fear
As he said: "Boy and man, you have known me,
  My friends, for this nigh forty year.

And you scarce may expect a confession
  Of error from me—but—you know
My dearly loved wife died last Christmas—
  It's now over ten months ago.
The winter went by long and lonely—
  But the springtime crep' forward apace,
The farm work begun, and I needed
  A woman, about the old place.

My children were wilder than rabbits,
  And all growing worse every day;
I could find no help in the village,
  Although I was willing to pay.
I declare I was near 'bout discouraged,
  And everything looked so forlorn,
When good little Patience McAlpine
  Skipped into our kitchen one morn.

She had only run in of an errand,
  But she laughed at our woe-begone plight,
And set to work just like a woman,
  A putting the whole place to rights.
And though her own folks was so busy,
  And illy her helpin' could spare,
She'd flit in and out like a sparrow,
  And most every day she was there.

So the summer went by, sort o' cheerful;
  But, one night, my baby, my Joe,
Was restless and feverish, and woke me,
  As babies will often, you know.
I was tired with my day's work and sleepy,
  And couldn't no way keep him still;
So at last I grew angry, and spanked him,
  And then he screamed out, with a will.

'Twas just then I heard a soft rapping
  Away at the half-open door—
And then little Patience McAlpine
  Stepped shyly across the white floor.
Says she : 'I thought Josie was crying;
  I guess I'd best take him away;
I knew you'd be getting up early
  To go to the marshes for hay.

So I staid here to-night, to get breakfast;
  I guess he'll be quiet with me;
Come, baby, kiss papa and tell him
  What a nice little man he will be.'
She was bending low over the baby—
  And saw the big tears on his cheek;
But her face was so near to my whiskers
  I daresn't move, scarcely, or speak.

Her arms were both holding the baby,
  Her eyes by his shoulder was hid—
But her mouth was so near and so rosy
  That—I kissed her—that's just what I did."
Then down sat the trembling sinner :
  The sisters they murmured "For shame!"
And " She shouldn't oughter a let him;
  No doubt *she* was mostly to blame."

When slowly uprose Deacon Pryor.
    "Now brethren *and* sisters," he said;
(And we knowed then that suthin' was coming,
    And we sot as still as the dead.)
"We've heard Brother Hartley's confession,
    And, I speak for myself, when I say,
That if my wife was dead, and my children
    Were all growing wuss every day;

"And if my house needed attention,
    And Patience MacAlpine should come
And tidy the cluttered-up kitchen,
    And make the place seem more like home—
And if I was tired out and sleepy,
    And my baby wouldn't lie still,
But cried out at midnight and woke me,
    As babies, we know, sometimes will;

"And if Patience came in to hush him,
    And 'twas all as our good brother says,
I think, friends—I think I should kiss her,
    And abide by the consequences."
Then down sat the elderly deacon;
    The younger one lifted his face,
And a smile rippled over the meeting,
    Like light in a shadowy place.

Perhaps, then, the matronly sisters
    Remembered their far-away youth,
Or the daughters at home by their firesides,
    Shrined each in her shy, modest truth.
For their judgments grew gentle and kindly;
    And—well! as I started to say,
The solemn old bells in the steeple,
    Were ringing a bridal to-day.

* * * * * *

Then Grandsire shook his head, and laughed, until
The tears filled all the furrows of his face;
And Grandma sighed, and said: "I thought old age
Would quench the fire of fun that with such zest
Has all your life long burned within your breast."
Then while they fell to talking of the news;
And who was dead or married; or what need
Existed for Church discipline; with whom,
Aunt Margaret slipped into another room,
And called for Prissie Hart: "Where are you, dear,
And what have you been doing this last hour?"
Prissie came forward in her shy, sweet way,
And sang a song, with "Here I am, dear aunt!"

"Wishing."

I was hiding in the parlor,
    Dreaming out the Christmas eve,
Listening idly to the children
    Their vague web of wishing weave.

They are such a merry party,
    Lu and Jasper, Fred and Claire,
And our youngest, Little Glory,
    With her shining golden hair.

Claire spoke first; she wished some fay might
    Weave for her a ribbon blue,
And about her white neck clasp it,
    With a diamond clear as dew.

Lu (the sturdy little Brownie)
    Wished no trinket at her throat,
But she wanted place to stand in,
    Power to speak, and right to vote.

Fred for books alone petitioned ;
    Jasper for a red roan steed ;
Was the little one a dreaming,
    That she gave their words no heed?

No! at last her wish was spoken,
    While her eyes looked large and bright :
"There are just two splendid people
    I wish I could see to-night."

"Who are they?" the others questioned,
    And, with hushed and reverent pause,
Little Glory answered softly,
    " They are Dod, and Santa Claus."
    *   *   *   *   *   *
"But, Auntie, tell us all a story! do!"

"No! you must tell me one. I want to hear
About your pleasant life."
                          "I have no skill
At story-telling craft, but sister Nan
Is always ready with some lively talk ;
Let's call on her." Nannette shook back her hair,
"I'll tell you, if you'll listen long and well,
    A true Thanksgiving story."
                          So she told,

X.

COUSIN NANNETTE'S STORY.

[ONE THANKSGIVING.]

OUT in the beautiful country,
  When the yellow moon was high,
When the Autumn fruits were garnered,
  And the Winter nights were nigh,

Old Farmer Pratt was counting
  His herds of lowing kine,
His sheep with growing fleeces,
  His lazy, fattened swine;

And, as he reckoned slowly,
  The calm and frosty night
Called him to barn and sheepfold,
  To see if all was right.

Under a sheltering hay-rick
  He paused to muse awhile,
When two young voices near him
  Awoke a passing smile:

One was his eldest daughter,
  Priscilla, speaking low,
And the other was one of the neighbors,
  He guessed, but he did not know.

"I can't!" Priscilla was saying,
  "I can't! it's going too far;
It would make me doubly wretched
  To be deceiving ma.

And father "—he felt the shudder
  That he could not hear or see;
And he said, "I b'lieve Priscilla
  Is fairly afraid of me.

She's a skeery thing, like her mother;
  But I vow I didn't suppose
The words I've said so keerless
  Was goin' home so close.

I've laughed about Reuben, and called him
  A sort of a shiftless lad,
But I never supposed the fellow
  Was anything very bad.

It seems he's been coaxin' and teasin'
  My Prissie to run away;
It can't do no harm, (I'm her father,)
  To listen to what they say.

If he gives her up for fear o' me,
  I don't think much o' him,
And I wonder, should she lose him,
  Would it make her bright eyes dim?"

"Priscilla, darling," 'twas Reuben,
  Speaking soft and low—
"I've waited in hope and patience
  Two weary years, you know,

And loved you as only a man loves
    The woman he means to wed;
And only for your sake, Prissie,
    No word have I ever said

To any one on the subject;
    But to-night—now, listen, dear!
We must have this matter settled;
    I can't wait another year.

I'll talk with your father to-morrow,
    And learn his objections to me."
"Oh, no!" said Priscilla in terror,
    For then he would think that we—

That I—had been talking about him,
    And that makes him angriest of all."
Then Reuben's voice grew firmer,
    And seemed to clearer fall:

"Your father is not an ogre;
    I do not dread his wrath,
'Tis better for us to be honest,
    And keep a straightforward path.

But I know what a faint-hearted chicken
    You are, and have always been,
And though I believe your father
    Is one of the best of men,

If he hates me as bad as you think for,
    Of course, he'll refuse outright,
All consent to our future wedding,
    And leave us no chance for flight;

For you never would dare to marry
    Right in the face and eyes
Of his plain commands against it,
    Though they be neither kind nor wise.

I've nothing to say of your parents,
    They're honest, and true, and good,
And you've served them and loved and obeyed them,
    As a dutiful daughter should.

But I've made up my mind to one thing:
    If you persistently say
That I mustn't speak to your father,
    Why, then, we must run away."

" Oh, Reuben!"   " Now Prissie, darling,
    I leave it to you to choose,
I've lost my heart and my patience,
    But my wife I'm not willing to lose.

I shan't discuss the subject
    By another word to-night,
But the day before Thanksgiving,
    If everything's fair and bright,

I'll hitch up my roan colt Major,
    And drive to the village, and see
If old Parson Emerson's willing
    To do a favor for me.

And then, when the stars are shining—"
    The young folks moved away,
And old Farmer Pratt stared, dumbly,
    With his head against the hay.

Next morning he watched Priscilla,
   Her blue eyes were swimming in tears,
And her quivering chin told plainly
   That her heart was full of fears.

Sometimes she'd look so earnest,
   As though she had something to say;
Then the tears would seem to choke her,
   And she'd turn her head away.

But the day before Thanksgiving
   Dawned crisp and bright and clear,
And every farmer's kitchen
   Was crowded with good cheer.

All day the wide brick ovens
   Were kept at pie-bake heat,
And merry voices echoed
   To the tread of busy feet.

All day the golden cider
   Slow trickled from the mill,
And all day long the farmer
   Was thinking, thinking still;

Towards night he jammed his hat on
   With most unusual vim,
And went across the meadow
   At a rapid stride, for him.

And then, ten minutes later,
   He paused beside a door
That he left in bitter anger
   Some fifteen years before.

Out stepped a cheery matron :
"Why, Brother Pratt ! You here ?
I'm sure I'm glad to see you ;
  Walk in and take a cheer.

The weather's getting chilly.
  How is your wife this fall ?
I often see your boys round,
  Handsome, and strong, and tall."

And so she chatted lightly,
  With deft, unconscious air,
And never even hinted
  'Twas strange to see him there.

But while he questioned to himself
  If she'd take Reuben's part,
The outer door swung slowly,
  And in walked Deacon Hart ;

No angry words were spoken,
  But Farmer Pratt learned then
That the plan he had discovered
  Was all unknown to them ;

The young folks asked no favors ;
  They knew an old feud lay
Smouldering between the fathers ;
  So they would run away.

But when the two men parted
  Beside the meadow stile,
Both faces wrinkled kindly
  With a grim and sober smile.

Hours after came the roan colt,
  Shaking his handsome head,
The bells were off the harness,
  And he seemed to lightly tread.

Priscilla hushed her sobbing,
  And hurried down the stair;
But just as she was stepping
  Out into the frosty air,

The kitchen-door flew open,
  Two tallow-dips ablaze
Filled her with sudden terror,
  And Reuben with amaze;

But her father's voice was calling:
  "Here, John, you hurry now—
Go get the ewe and cossets;
  Drive round the brindle cow;

Roll out that barrel of apples,
  And the white Chenangoes fine;
And bring a keg of cider,
  And a jug of currant wine.

Willie, tie up the feather bed,
  And put the pillows in;
And, mother, where's the pillow-slips,
  And sheets and quilts and things?

Bring out the new rose blankets
  That in the clothes-press lay;
Prissie must have her setting out—
  She's going to run away."

Imagine all the wonder
    . That from this was sure to come !
Imagine tears and kisses
    Thrown in *ad libitum !*

And two shame-faced young people
    Waiting another day,
And then concluding quietly
    They wouldn't run away.

The happiest Thanksgiving
    That e'er New England knew
Dawned on the village homes next day,
    Where hearts beat warm and true.

Old feuds were all forgotten—
    Old troubles lain aside—
And Reuben lived to bless the day
    He won his happy bride.

*   *   *   *   *   *

Aunt Margaret, laughing merrily, spoke out :
"Oh, Nan, you bad, bad girl ! Poor Prissie's face
Is pinker than a rose.
                        Whose turn comes next ?"
"Oh, let the children say their verses now,"
Said Cousin Nan—adding, *sotto voce*,
" I've drilled them to within a half an inch
Of their dear lives, and yet I warrant you
That every one of them will miss two-thirds
Of all I meant for them to say. Come, Claire ! "
Claire drew her tiny figure up, and spoke
As easily as though she thought the world
Was made for her especial heritage :
" As story-telling is the rule this eve,

I'll tell my story of a little girl,
Whose parents died while she was yet a babe,
And left her to her grandsire's tender care ;
A quaint old German basket-maker, he."

LITTLE MACHEN.

"Up a few steps higher, Machen,
    Only up anoder flight ;
Are your little feet aweary
    Mit der walk dey took to-night ?

Ah, you could not sell der baskets,
    And your very step is sad.
Come and sing to me, my darling,
    It will make my old heart glad.

Yes ! your voice is growing stronger ;
    It was always sweet and clear ;
Softly, Machen, sing more softly,
    Lest some one outside should hear.

Now remember what I tell you,
    Never sing a vord or note
On d' street or in d' alley ;
    Keep der song-birds in your throat ;

Keep them all for me, my Machen ;
    Never mind if we are poor ;
We will never sell our music
    For der money, dat is sure.

Sing again ! Your voice revives me
    Like a draught of cool, red wine,
And I seem to hear der echoes
    Of d' falling of d' Rhine.

Hand me down my dear old viol,
    Let me hear it wailing low;
I shall e'en forget my blindness,
    It will charm avay my woe;

Dear! you know der rent is heavy,
    And we move to-morrow night,
Up anoder story, Machen,
    Only up anoder flight."

Little Machen listened sadly,
    To her Grandsire's rambling talk;
True it was, her feet were weary
    With her long and fruitless walk;

And her heart was full of trouble,
    For their little store of gold
Lessened slowly, lessened surely,
    As the passing days were told;

She could count the landlord's visits
    By the plaintive news at night:
"Up anoder story, Machen,
    Only up anoder flight."

"I am going, little Machen;"
    Grandsire's voice was weak and low;
"I was wrong to hush d' song-birds
    In your throat—dey warble so,

Dey would bring you food, and fortune,
    Dey would bring you gold, and gear;
Ah, 'tis late! too late, my Machen,
    Hush! your mutter's voice I hear,

Come to guide me on my journey,
    To her home of love and light;
Up a little higher, Machen,
    Only up anoder flight."

Years went by; a glorious singer,
    Makes a million hearts rejoice,
With her life's pure, quiet beauty,
    And the magic of her voice.

And we know her music thrills us
    With such wondrous power to-night,
Just because her heart is always
    Ready for higher flight.

    *   *   *   *   *   *

"Well done, dear girlie!" Grandma softly says;
But Nan is in a hurry;—she breaks in:
"Now, Lu—you good folks please to understand
Lu is thirteen, and studies woman's rights;
She wrote her piece for some school festival."
Lu stood by Auntie and recited thus:

THE QUESTION.

Schoolmates—girls, I mean,—one question
    Rises now to be discussed;
And I think, if we *can* meet it,
    That we ought to, and we must.

It has reference to our future,
    And it tells us, plain and true,
That, whatever may surround us,
    We, ourselves, have work to do.

True, we may have friends, to guide us,
    They, with love, our paths may pave,
And our homes may be kept safe, by
    Father strong, and brothers brave.

But, when father's brow grows furrowed,
    And his hair with silver blended,
Then we know too well how soon his
    Earthly journey may be ended.

And our brothers care far more
    (Though they may not be unkind)
For some other fellow's sister
    Than their own, we often find.

More than this, we know a lesson,
    Taught us in our early youth,
That, though words may be mistaken,
    Figures always speak the truth.

And the truth is not a secret;
    For the stern statistics say
There are seventy thousand women
    More than men alive, to-day,

In the limits of New England;
    And the Bay State has her share,
Counting, as her steady surplus,
    Forty thousand daughters fair.

Girls, this may seem a misfortune;
    But,—old things must pass away,
And we'll hold a large majority
    Of votes, some coming day.

Therefore, let us never falter
In the path of education,
For our truth and trust may yet be
The salvation of the nation.

And through any storm or sunshine
One plain fact we'll keep in view,
That whatever may surround us,
We, ourselves, have work to do.

*   *   *   *   *   *

Lu had her generous share of praise, be sure;
But soon Aunt Nan, impatient, called, "Here, Fred!"
And Fred brushed up his sunny hair, and said:
"Friends, if I must apologize, my 'piece'
Is very local in significance;
'Twas written when our town gave up her name,
And took another, prettier, we think."

"WAKEFIELD."

In a time long since departed,
So the ancient legends tell us,
Came a handful of brave workers,
Sturdy men and women, true.
And they built a little hamlet,
Close beside a brawling river,
Where the "waterfalls" were plenty,
Though the silken gowns were few.

First a dozen log-built houses,
Then a church, and then a saw-mill,
Then a school-house, for the children
Grow, like field-flowers, everywhere;

Then the half-fledged baby village
Must be christened; in due order;
And their truant hearts turned backward
To old England, stern but fair.

Wide and wild the little township
Stretched away o'er hill and meadow,
And they called the clearing Reading,
For the home across the sea;
And their children's children's children
Scattered; founded other hamlets;
And, by adding points of compass
Grew, like one great family;

Reading West, and North, and South, too,
Daughters of old mother Reading.
But a change comes o'er the spirit
Of the matron's household dream,
For her youngest child has vanished,
Like the "Ancient Arrow Maker's,"
And *South Reading* lives no longer
Save in memory's fading gleam.

In the fairest pillared mansion
That ere graced our lake's green border,
Where no childish footsteps fall on
Terraced walk or marble pave,
Where the pea-fowls flaunt their gorgeous plumes
 And tropic blossoms brighten,
There, there lives our noble patron,
Who this patronymic gave.

And in honoring his bounty,
May we each, as faithful students,

Wake to fields of progress brighter
Than we've ever known before;
And with thanks to Mother Reading
For her early care and training,
Heart and voice we turn to Wakefield;
Wakefield now and evermore.

* * * * * *

"Three cheers for Wakefield;" shouted Cousin Tom;
And every boy rings out a lusty cheer
As if to air his lungs. "Now, Jasper dear."
Aunt Nan's fond look of happy pride tells well,
Which child among them all she loves the best;
She puts her arm about him, as he says:

THE WALKING DOLL.

Did you think it was fashioned of wax or of wood,
    With a main-spring inside to be wound with a key?
Did you think it would turn round its bright little head,
    And smile upon you, as it smiles upon me?

I saw how politely you lifted your hat,
    And I guessed at the sneer that your lip let fall;
You were chatting of her at the club, last night,
    And you called her—I heard you—a "Walking Doll."

You are counting the cost of her dresses, you say,
    And you scold that her style is so faultlessly calm;
You hint that a crown would look well on her brow,
    And a sceptre rest light in her firm rosy palm.

But her heart is as true as her beauty is fair,
    And her warm blush comes quick at a fond whisper's call,
And a story of trouble or sorrow will bring
    Two tears to the eyes of that "Walking Doll!"

By the way ! did I tell you ?   A card for you here !
   A reception next Wednesday.   Oh yes, I shall go.
You had better look in ; no ! there'll not be a crowd ;
   At three hundred and twenty ! her father's, you know.

Well, yes !   There's a wedding that morning at ten ;
   The reception is later.   Now, don't fail to call,
For the fact is—the fact is—don't stare so, old friend,
   I'm going to marry that "Walking Doll."
             *   *   *   *   *   *
Aunt Nannette stared as though she thought the boy
Had taken sudden leave of all his wits ;
His father laughed !   " You quizzical young rogue,
Where did you learn that bit of nonsense ; say !
Can't you repeat the pretty New Year's rhymes,
Aunt Margaret wrote, a long long time ago,
Before your Uncle Willie went to Heaven ? "
Then the spoiled Laddie shrugged his shoulders up,
And spoke again.

THE SNOW-STORM.

"With never a plume by the wind set humming,"
The snow has come and still is coming,
Soft and slow, through the pathless air,
Like millions of messenger birdlings fair.

Floating with measureless, matchless grace,
Through the mystical, cloud-circled, silvery space,
And the children are planning with boisterous zeal
Some sport for the morrow as children will.

But John, a young gentleman, turns away
With impatient words from their merry play,

And looks with half-angry, regretful eyes,
At the cool soft gray of the sunset skies.

For John is intending, to-morrow, to ride,
With his lady fair, down to Ingleside;
And he vows that to usher the New Year in,
With that nasty storm, seems a deuced sin.

Stephen laughs loudly, and shakes his head,
As he ties a new rope to his half-worn sled;
Prissie grows pink 'neath her hair's sunny gleam,
As sleigh-bells and moonlight enliven her dream.

Nan hums a song, and her eyes flash bright,
As she rattles her skates with impatient delight;
But dear little Willie turns round in his chair,
Saying gravely, "Oh! John, you should be 'shamed to swear.

On'y see how the dirty black road grows white;
The Angels are shedding their fedders to-night;
Shedding their fedders to keep us warm,
They don't know it's a nasty storm."

Darling Willie! Our household joy;
John stands rebuked by the sober-faced boy,
Mother bends low with a kiss for her pet,
And he wonders what makes his forehead wet.

But the wild North wind that is rising and humming,
And the snow that has come, and still is coming,
Bring a deeper peace and a kindlier rest
For the quaint sweet thought by the child expressed.

* * * * * *

Then Uncle Christopher's Laurette drew near,
Joined the gay group, and told a story bright,
Of a defiant, brave-eyed country-girl,
Who valued patriotism more than pride,
And gave her handsome city lover up,
Because he shirked his duty, as she thought.

XI.

COUSIN LAURETTE'S STORY.

[WILL, MY BROTHER.]

WILL, my brother, has bright blue eyes,
   And his high white brow is broad and fair,
And seventeen summers have clipped and browned
   The golden curls that he used to wear.

But Claude, my lover, has eyes of jet,
   And hair like the gloss of the raven's plume;
His lips are redder than coral, wet,
   And his cheek is dark, with its bearded bloom.

And Claude is twenty-seven years old;
   A *man* on Wall Street's crowded mart,
With his scheming brain and his gleaming gold;
   But little Will is a man, in heart.

For when far and wide had the summons flown,
   "*Men to arms!* for your country's sake!"
"Liberty totters upon her throne!"
   "Freedom is jeopardized!" "Right at stake!"

Though Claude belonged to the First Brigade,
   And held a Lieutenant's commission too,
Though he liked the glitter of dress parade,
   Yet there came a rumor, whence, none knew,

That he had decided not to go ;
  Had taken his name from the company's roll,
Resigned his commission and left the ranks.
  Oh, Claudius ! Claudius ! where was your soul ?

But I spurned the thought that he feared to die,
  So I fashioned shirts of the softest wool ;
And knit such socks as no wealth could buy,
  And stitched upon each his name in full,

And waited and watched, day after day ;
  Upon the morrow the troops would start ;
And the lagging hours could scarce keep pace
  With the weary throbs of my anguished heart.

But he came, at last ! In the twilight gloom,
  When the busy cares of the day were o'er ;
He came from his far away city home,
  And sat him down by my father's door.

The hand that I gave him grew cold with fear,
  And his welcoming kiss touched a tear-wet cheek ;
I shuddered to think of our parting, so near,
  And chided my fond heart for being so weak.

But what were the words he said, think you ?
  As we sat alone by the parlor grate ?
Why ! that all the story I'd heard was true,
  And to leave home, now, would be tempting fate.

" For you know," he remarked, with a glance of pride,
  " 'Tis not as though I were a laboring man ;
I have gold to win for my promised bride,
  And work to do that no other can."

At first I listened with speechless scorn,
   To the soft excuses he murmured o'er ;
Then I called him "a coward," "a traitor born,"
   And bade him leave me forevermore.

And Claude, my lover, grew angry then,
   And cursed a " Yankee girl's swerveless grit ; "
I tossed him a taunt for "New York men,"
   And thus we parted—" Peace follow it."

Next morn down the staircase came brother Will,
   Wearing his uniform dress throughout ;
His graceful figure looked slighter still,
   But his heart was brave and strong, no doubt.

I gave him the package of clothes I had wrought
   For a taller form and a stronger arm ;
His face grew dark with a troubled thought,
   But he said, " I take them ; a sister's charm."

Then he added proudly, "You know my place,
   I am standard-bearer for ' Company A,'
And I never held our beautiful flag
   With a firmer hand than I shall to-day."

" Father ! your blessing is all I crave.
   Mother ! one kiss ! and now, good-by.
No nobler bed than a soldier's grave
   I ask, when my country calls to die."

O Claude, my lover, to-night has pressed
   His beautiful couch in his marble home ;
While Will, my brother, lies down to rest,
   Wrapped in his blanket, 'neath Heaven's blue dome.

And which in the great All Father's sight
   Does best the mission of man fulfil?
Which walks nearest to God and the right—
   Claude, my lover, or brother Will?

   *   *   *   *   *   *

"They were not lovers," murmured Cousin Bess.
"She did not love him, or she never could
Have given him up so easily."
                        "Oh, fie,"
Said Cousin Kittie. "Don't talk sentiment,
I'd rather hear war stories, even though
They must be sad. I'll tell you now about
Little boy blue—Aunt Betsey's sister's boy."

CHARLIE.

"The boys are going to enlist,"
   Cried Charlie; "and to-day
I'll put *my* name down next to theirs;
   Say, father, if I may?'

But father only shook his head,
   And answered very slow:
"You're such a little, pale-faced boy,
   They'll never let you go.

"Why, Will is twenty-four years old,
   And 'Liab scarcely less;
Just fit to rough it in the camp;
   They'll stand it well, I guess."

"But, father, I am strong, you know,
   And growing older fast;"
And so with many eager words
   The cause was won at last.

And Charlie, o'er whose slender form
    Scarce seventeen years have fled,
With Will and 'Liab sleeps to-night
    Upon his soldier bed.

The sturdy Germans rise as though
    'Twere Faderland at stake,
And Erin's jolly sons pour forth
    For Mother Countrie's sake.

And more—our pale-browed Yankee boys
    Leave home and school and farm,
To face a cruel enemy,
    Mid every kind of harm.

Therefore we know, though foreign hearts
    Are stout and arms are strong,
We can depend on native strength
    To right our country's wrong.

God keep thee, Charlie. Danger ne'er
    Shall dim thy laughing eye,
Or steal the dimples from thy cheek,
    Or make thee fear to die,

And while our troubled country needs
    The strength of thy right arm,
We know thy brave heart will not shrink
    From any coming harm.

    *   *   *   *   *   *

Poor Charlie! He came home all wearied out,
With camp and march and sound of battle strife,
And kissed his mother, and just drooped and died.

Then some young urchin told of

CORPORAL JIM.

He bade us farewell with a droll, sober smile,
That told us how fearless his heart felt, the while ;
But he said when he left us : " I never shall write,
Come murder or mercy, come frolic or fight ;
So don't watch the mails till your dear eyes grow dim."
Oddest of mortals is Corporal Jim.

We sent him a box full of treasures, one day,
Which he shared with his messmates in his sober way.
"And now," cried the boys, "you will certainly write
To acknowledge the gift that has reached us to-night."
" Oh, the candles are out, and the camp-fires are dim ;
You don't catch me writing," laughed Corporal Jim.

But we know, in his heart, he was breathing a prayer
Of thanks for New England, and cherished friends there.
Though southward his feet and his fancies may roam,
He will not forget that the Northland is home.
His few quiet words are sufficient for him,
We're willing to wait for you, Corporal Jim.

* * * * * *

In quick response came quiet Cousin Jim
Who told a story of his soldier life ;
While all the little ones were kissed "good-night !"
And borne upstairs and tucked away in bed.

Then Cousin Tom pretended he had found
Nannette's portfolio, and from that he read

ANNIVERSARY EVE.

'Twas just such a night as this
  Not a thousand winters ago,
I sat in this very parlor dim,
Watching the moonbeams flickering in,
  And the firelight's steadier glow.

And there was another here;
  Oh memory full of pain;
The words he whispered so low in mine ear
I fancied the angels might smile to hear,
  While the old clock throbbed a refrain.

He asked, "Will my Nannie walk
  By my side through our coming life?
Will you lay your beautiful hands in mine,
Through the winter's chill and the summer's shine,
  And be my bride, my wife?"

With never a thought of fear
  I answered him, sober and true;
"Life is lonely and dark and drear,
Love is sweet and friends are dear—
  Allan, I'll go with you."

Then he placed on my finger white
  My blue betrothal ring,
And bade me wear it until my life
Was merged in his; his bride, his wife,
  Whatever fate might bring.

Oh, ring in thy velvet case!
With thy diamond eye gleaming still,
Oh, cruel lover, with all thy grace!
Sad, sad is the memory-haunted place
In my weary heart, that ye fill.

God pity thee! faithless one!
God pity thy fair young bride!
Her life will be darkened forevermore
By the curse that lieth at thy heart's door,
Thy perjury and thy pride.
* * * * * *
The cousins, looking at each other, said:
"Who would believe that merry-eyed Nannette
Had ever known such trouble as that tells?"
But Tom read on:
Here is another bit
She calls " Profitless Work"—Let's see what 'tis.

PROFITLESS WORK.

"I have been spinning, Allan,
    Spinning a golden thread,
Rarely bright—and the spinning-wheel
    Was only my foolish head.
Only the wild, sweet fancies
    Of my happy heart and brain,
Forming themselves into visions
    That never may come again.
And I have been weaving, Allan,
    Weaving my thread of gold."
* * * * * *
"Now, Cousin Nettie," called Nannette's gay voice,
"Or you or Cousin Tom, no more excuse
Will we accept from either one of you."

"I've said my verses," promptly answered Tom,
Hiding the stolen paper out of sight,
"While you were off upstairs.   They read like this :

THE FADED ROSE.

I overturned my writing desk
   And found—oh, pity me !
The pale ghost of a buried love
   I never thought to see.

I grasped it as the miser grasps
   His hoarded golden ore,
And scorned myself for touching it,
   And only held it more.

A lover's gift, a faded rose
   Pinned to a tiny sheet,
On which he wrote, " I'm coming soon,
   Your waiting lips to greet.

Don't watch your eyes out, darling,
   For the lighted evening train,
You'll see me when the Sabbath bells,
   Ring out their sweet refrain."

And so he came !   How memory paints
   That long, bright summer day ;
And all the loving words he spoke
   In the hours we dreamed away.

Weak, foolish words ; I thought they were
   Forgotten long ago,
When first I learned their teachery,
   And reeled beneath the blow.

Oh glistening wealth, oh golden lure,
　　You tempted his vain pride,
I thought he counted love worth more
　　Than all the world beside.

But I would not that his pretty wife
　　Should guess what bonds he brake,
Or know the cruel wrong he wrought
　　For less than her sweet sake.

Then stay, old rose—I'll keep you now
　　Lest some day, who knows who
May speak such fond sweet words as those,
　　And I believe them true.

　　*　　*　　*　　*　　*　　*

Nannette flushed painfully, and turned away.
But Tom puts out a pleading, coaxing hand :
" O Cousin, don't be angry, for you know
I would not hurt your feelings for the world.
Forgive me, please, and I'll hunt up for you
A reminiscence of my vanished youth."
" Don't do it, Tom," Aunt Prudence gravely says,
" Your youth time was quite bad enough at best;
And, having passed, you'd better let it rest."
" Now, Auntie, if you hadn't said a word,"
Tom answers quick, " I wouldn't have betrayed
Your influence upon my early life ;
I'll do it now. So listen, for here goes :

XII.

COUSIN TOM'S STORY.

[YOUTHFUL EXPERIENCE.]

AUNT PRUE was a little particular,
   And I was a little gay,
So when she caught me doing things
   She thought were out of the way—

She'd drive me into a corner
   With her questions, cute and clear,
And sometimes, dodge or no dodge
   I couldn't quite keep clear.

At last, when I grew a big fellow,
   A score of years or so,
I fell in love with a beauty;
   Her name was Nettie Snow.

'Twas then Aunt Prue made manifest
   Her righteous Baptist ire;
For Nettie sang first treble
   In the Unitarian choir.

She told me all the awful texts
   A Parson ere could show forth
About "the unbelieving soul;"
   "Be ye not yoked," and so forth;

'Till she thought the thing was settled
  Beyond a chance for doubt;
But I hankered after Nettie
  And this was what came about:

One day, in the hottest weather,
  (I won't forget it soon,
The Baptist meeting was over
  Quite early, that afternoon,)

Aunt Prue heard a sound of music,
  That throbbed on the summer air,
So she stole in softly, to listen
  To the Unitarian choir.

Unconscious of any danger,
  I stood by Nettie's side,
My soul on her voice floating outward,
  Like a barque on a sunny tide.

And after the benediction,
  I lingered to see her home,
And loitered, and talked, and murmured,
  'Till the stars began to come.

Then I hurried me home to supper;
  Aunt Prue, with a quiet air,
Asked, "Tom, do you know who sings tenor
  In the Unitarian choir?"

I thought perhaps some one had told her
  That I had been there that day;
So I said—"It's a fellow who looks like me,
  But what his name is, I can't say."

Said she—That fellow who looks like you
    Must have borrowed your coat to wear,
And she took from my tell-tale shoulder
    A long, bright golden hair.

Well! I found Aunt Prue was worried,
    And so for a time I tried
To give up all thoughts of Nettie,
    At least as my future bride.

But the old love was earnest and faithful,
    I could not persuade it to die;
I wanted to see my treasure
    Once more; just to say good-by.

So I went with Aunt Prue to the Baptists
    All day, (Good boy, you see,)
And when she was reading her hymn-book
    In the parlor after tea—

I did not wait for permission,
    As you may well suppose,
But I took a bee-line through the meadows
    On my way to Dr. Snow's.

And soon I peeped in at the window,
    And who do you think was there?
Why, my cousin John a-sitting,
    As straight as a cob, in a chair.

His best Sunday-meeting clothes on,
    He looked well enough; but then,
If some one had routed that fellow,
    How glad I'd have said Amen.

But Nettie, the blessed angel,
   Her face flushed pink with surprise;
I knew she was glad to see me,
   By the curious look in her eyes.

We chatted till John grew angry;
   "I guess I'll be going, said he;"
And I feared the old folks would scold her,
   For they liked him better than me.

So I said, "I'd go too," and together
   We climbed the old meadow stile;
And he said "he had just concluded
   To go out West, for awhile."

I tried to express my sorrow,
   And "wished I was going too;"
But I was religiously lying,
   A fact which he very well knew.

Soon after he left us, the young folks
   Were going to ride one day;
I wanted to go and take Nettie,
   So I studied and planned a way.

The morning came; I was shaving,
   And Odin was cutting around;
A ten-year-old, fuller of mischief
   Than a church-bell is of sound.

I thought I must hear from Nettie,
   So I told him to go to see
If she was getting ready,
   And be sure to call her *he.*—

For I was determined Aunt Prudence
  Should think I had gone with a man;
"Oh, yes," said the good-natured monkey,
  "I'll hurry as fast as I can."

Off he went, and was back in a jiffy;
  I asked: "Well, what did he say?"
"*He* said, 'he was almost ready;
  He is glad it's a pleasant day.'"

"And what was *he* doing?" Aunt Prue asked,
  With such a grave, innocent air,
I knew my poor trick was discovered;
  I was angry enough to swear.

"He was, ah! he was, ma'am! he was, ah!"
  I strangled myself with a cough;
"He was just putting on *his* new bonnet;"
  And the mischievous imp ran off.

I sank down, as weak as a baby;
  She'd up and tell grandsire, of course,
And then, he could keep me from going,
  By fussing about the horse.

I was sulkily thinking it over;
  There was not a word to be said,
I hated myself so badly;
  When a hand fell light on my head.

I looked up; Aunt Prue's eyes were smiling;
  "My foolish boy," said she,
"If you find that new bonnet becoming,
  You'd better ask *him* home to tea."

Dear, patient, long-suffering Auntie,
  She never would teaze me again ;
My heart brimmed over with gladness,
  And whispered, Amen, Amen.

She knew that nor creed nor doctrine,
  Two loving young hearts should divide ;
And now, you all want me to tell you,
  How fair Nettie looked as a bride ?

Well, yes ; she was married next spring-time,
  Aunt Prue knows just how she was drest ;
And I was the bridegroom ?   Not any !
  'Twas my cousin John, from the West.
      *   *   *   *   *   *
The hearty echoing laugh, that once or twice
Had broken up the solemn monotone
Of Cousin Tom's recital, rang again
As he ceased speaking, and the girls cried out,
" Oh, what a shame for you to cheat us so
Of the one grain of romance, that we thought
Lay hidden in your story.   Surely, then,
You should have married Nettie."   " Well, perhaps,"
And Tom sighed mockingly.   " We never know
Just what we should do, dears."   And then he turned
With, " Who speaks next ? "   And dear Aunt Margaret
    said,
" There's John's wife crooning o'er her baby boy ;
I know she likes to chatter."
                          " After you,
Dear Auntie," pleaded pretty Mrs. John ;
And so Aunt Margaret, being hardly urged,
Tells us a story of her Southern life.

XIII.

AUNT MARGARET'S STORY.

[THE OCTOROON.]

IN the palmy days of slavery,
    A score of years ago,
A pretty, dark-skinned Octoroon,
    Was singing, soft and low,
A song, to please her baby,
    As in her arms it lay—
A dainty, dimpled, fair-haired boy,
    A twelvemonth old that day.

Strange home for child or woman;
    Her quick ear often heard,
Mid the click of dice and glasses,
    Many a loud and angry word.
For her Philip was a gambler;
    But she never dreamed or thought
Of any shame or sorrow
    For the wrong he might have wrought.

She called him "Phil," or "Philip,"
    "My man," sometimes "my boy,"
And took, in baby, home, and him,
    A woman's natural joy.
"He plays seven-up till midnight,"
    She often, laughing, told;
"And then, like other gentlemen,
    Comes home and counts his gold.

"Save when he's up the river
    On the Princess or Dian,
Then me and baby wait for him
    And do the best we can."
And he was always kind to her,
    He gave her jewels rare,
And praised her graceful figure,
    And her long and shining hair.

While she was always happy,
    Singing French songs sweet and wild,
With a voice as full of music
    As the laughter of a child.
But one midnight, she was waiting
    For his footstep on the stair,
Came a tramp of measured meaning,
    Throbbing on the silent air.

Came a sound of troubled voices,
    Filling all her heart with dread;
Comrades bearing up a burden,
    Cold and lifeless! Phil was dead!
Like a sudden blow it smote her
    With a desolate sense of grief;
No faintness came to shield her,
    And no tears to bring relief.

Oh! to escape that heart-ache,
    And the dumb, bewildering pain,
How gladly would she fall asleep,
    And never wake again;
Only baby must be cared for,
    He was Philip's baby still,
With his father's Saxon beauty,
    Her own darling little Phil.

Then she wondered, vaguely dreaming,
  As a weary child might do,
If her Philip left a heap of gold,
  For her, and baby too;
Still she watched, with heart near bursting,
  When they bore his form away,
Then she listened to the prosing
  Of two lawyers old and gray,

As they talked of debts of honor,
  Of the house and horses fine,
Of the furniture and jewelry,
  Of plate, perhaps, and wine;
Then! Ah then, what was the meaning
  Of the words they muttered o'er,
As they said the "Wench and baby
  Ought to bring a thousand more."

Quickened ear and comprehension
  Caught each careless tone and word;
Knew too well the tricks of trade, to
  Doubt the cruel truth she heard;
But when they so gruffly told her
  There would be a sale to-morrow,
Then her voice wailed out in
  Piteous cry of bitterness and sorrow.

"Oh! I know Phil never meant that
  Me and baby should be sold;
Why! I've been his 'little woman'
  Since I'se only twelve years old.
He won me from the Cap'en
  When they played sev'n-up one night;
An he's tole me more'n a thousand times
  He's sure to make it right.

The Cap'n was my father,
  Cap'n Winslow, of Belleaire;
And you can't sell me and baby—
  Oh! you can't, you'll never dare."
Those men, so used to suffering,
  And callous as they were,
Looked in each other's faces,
  And paused to pity her. .

But many a case was just as bad,
  And some perhaps were worse;
They could do nothing, any way,
  The law must take its course;
The broken-hearted mother tried,
  In vain, to sleep that night;
Her busy brain would conjure up
  Some possible means of flight.

She shuddered with a vision
  Of the bloodhounds on her track,
As she felt how deadly certain
  They would be to bring her back.
Then she thought of little Philip,
  As he slumbered in her arms,
With a burly-visaged trader
  Gloating o'er his baby charms.

Counting up the money value
  Of his sunny, waving hair,
Of his dainty lip's soft curving,
  And his brow so broad and fair.
Oh! She could not—could not bear it,
  She would kill herself and him.
But across her 'wildered memory
  Stole an echo, faint and dim,

Of some reverent childish teaching,
   Prayer to God, and faith and fear,
"Lead us not into temptation!"
   Was He list'ning? Did He hear?
Then she thought of old Aunt Dinah
   Who had taught her thus to pray,
Living, free, in Opelousas,
   Half a score of miles away.

Well she knew she was a prisoner,
   And the house was thronged with men;
But she knew, too, that for years the
   Place had been a gambler's den;
And a long, low, vaulted chamber
   Ran beneath the basement floor,
Opening far beyond detection
   In a heavy hidden door.

Quick as thought her heart decided
   That the danger should be braved;
Though her life should pay the forfeit,
   Little Philip would be saved.
For they would not heed or miss her
   Till the morning sun was high,
And she'd trust it all to Auntie;
   Any way, she could but die.

So she wrapped her sleeping treasure
   In a mantle dark and thin,
Tied a gaudy-hued bandanna
   'Neath her smoothly rounded chin,
Planned her flight to 'scape detection,
   And removing every trace,
With the supple, stealthy movement
   Of a leopard, left the place.

Soon the city lay behind her,
  And the country opened fair,
Bathed in beauty, with the moonlight
  Falling golden through the air.
But she paused not with her burden;
  Life or death still lay before,
Till she struggled, worn and weary,
  To Aunt Dinah's cabin door.

Hush! A voice of prayer and pleading,
  On the midnight calm, she heard:
"Teach us, Lord, through all our blindness
  To believe Thy precious Word;
Help us when our hearts are fainting,
  Guide us when we go astray,
Lead us in the paths we know not,
  Nearer to Thee, day by day."

With her prescient soul awakened,
  By the strange magnetic thrill,
That beyond the outer senses
  Whispers of some coming ill;
With her spirit vision opened
  By some viewless inner sight,
Old Aunt Dinah had arisen,
  And was praying in the night.

In her strong black arms she gathered
  Weary mother, wondering child,
And she listened to the story
  Full of anguish deep and wild,
Knowing well she could not save them;
  For her love, though strong and bright,
Was as chaff before the whirlwind,
  To the white man's power and might.

I would give my poor old heart's blood,
  Every drop, for yours and you,
If I could but keep you, honey,
  From this path yer walking through.
But I'se seen it all too often ;
  Dey will hunt yer if yer hide,
Dey will catch yer if yer fleeing,
  Dey will scourge yer from my side.

Dey will take yer baby from ye !
  Stop ! De Lord's own voice I hear !
Will yer trust yer precious treasure,
  To *my* care, and leave him here ?
I will keep him from all danger,
  Hide him where no eye can see,
And 'twill be a comfort, dearie,
  If you allers know he's free.

Fifty years I served my massa ;
  Toward the last he promised, sure,
I should have my freedom papers,
  And it helped me to endure ;
But I bore him twenty children,
  And while I've been growing old,
I have lived to see the last one
  Taken from me ; yes ! and sold.

Gladly would I give the remnant,
  Of my worn-out life to save
Either one of 'em, from being,
  Just for one short hour, a slave.
Don't look so ! Give me the baby !
  An' de moon is goin' down—
You mus' take my little donkey, chile,
  And hurry back to town.

Ride him jus' as fur's yer dare to,
  Den tie up de bridle rein,
Turn his head, and he's done sart'in
  To come right smart home again.
I will pray for you to-morrow;
  Yes! I know how hard it is;
But we do the Father's bidding,
  Not in our way, but in His."

Human nature shrank and quivered,
  But the mother heart was brave;
Giving up her child to freedom,
  Turning back herself a slave.
When, next morning, she was summoned
  From her room, she walked alone;
Though her soft brown eyes burned darkly,
  They were tearless, dry as stone.

And the lawyers, and the keepers,
  Looking at her crouched away,
Minded by her wondrous beauty,
  Of a tigress turned at bay;
But a query ran among them,
  Of the baby—"Where was he?"
Till she heard their words, and answered,
  Very calmly—"He is free."

Free? The house was strongly guarded,
  Every window, every door;
They had seen both child and mother,
  Safely caged the night before;
Not a human thing had ventured
  O'er the threshold, that they knew,
And the hounds, with hungry voices,
  Bayed outside, the whole night through.

Rapid search sufficed to show them
  That the youngling was not there ;
Neither hint, nor trace, nor clue,
  Could they discover anywhere.
Then, with threatening look and gesture,
  To the mother they returned ;
And she said, with voice triumphant,
  While her eyes still clearer burned,

"Strike me, minions, I expect it ;
  Scourge me, burn me, beat and kill,
But it will not help you find him ;
  He is free ! my darling Phil.
Think you I would fear to hide him
  In the darkness of the grave.
Ah ! my baby's father's baby
  Was not born to be a slave."

Superstitious, flushed with anger,
  Yet with terror turning pale,
Sudden, selfish interest told them
  It would hurt their chattel sale,
If the lash should sting her shoulders now,
  Or mar her graceful hips,
And they knew no pain or torture
  Could unseal a mother's lips.

So with furtive eyes they watched her,
  Talking loud 'tween fear and fright,
Half afraid, 'mid their bravado,
  She would vanish from their sight.
But she stood as stands the martyr
  When his last frail hope dies out,
And the murmuring sea of voices
  Rises to an awful shout ;

When he sees far off the fagots piled,
  The blazing torch beside,
And no kindly whisper greets him
  O'er that surging human tide.
Aye! she stood as stands the martyr
  Hedged about by cruel wrong,
Save that, as the martyr raises
  His triumphant voice in song,

All the ransomed harps of Heaven
  Tuned to welcome he can hear,
While the angels and archangels
  Seem to bend and hover near,
Bidding him be strong and patient
  Through his one brief hour of pain,
That the victor's palm and conqueror's
  Crown of glory he may gain.

But for her, alas! the auction block
  Was not a portal bright
Leading unto life eternal,
  Far beyond earth's dreary night.
It was but the gate to perils
  Which she knew not, could not know,
And a new life opened suddenly
  Before her, full of woe.

Truly she was dark but comely;
  Cooler blood or colder sky
Never could have lit the changeful fire
  That burned in her dark eye.
Never with such rare vermilion
  Could have touched her lips soft red,
Or on cheek and brow such rosy
  Tints of brown and amber spread.

But she thought not of her beauty,
  As her heart beat fast and faster,
Gazing on those stranger faces,
  Wond'ring which would be her master.
Scarce she heard the slow bids lagging,
  Or the auctioneer's last call,
Heeded scarce the breathless silence,
  Or the hammer's clinking fall.

But the horrid truth awoke her:
  Going! Going! Gone! it told,
That beyond all hope or dreaming
  She was sold—to slavery! Sold.

*   *   *   *   *   *

"Come, children, children," Grandma's voice breaks in,
"Your auntie's story makes your eyes too bright,
Those troublous times are long since passed away,
It is not well to dwell upon them now."
"Oh! please, Aunt Margaret, tell us more," they say,
  "Tell us if she was treated kindly, do.
And did the little Philip grieve and die
Because he lost his mother? Did she ne'er
See his sweet face again"—oh tell us more.

"Yes, dears, I'll tell you briefly what befell
The pretty Marian,—and how she fared.
A trader bought her—I have heard them tell
His name—I think they called him Captain Moore.
But soon he found some legal fault or flaw,
By which his claim was open to dispute;
He dared not sell her for the liberal price
He hoped to gain, and so he talked with her,
Telling her, if she chose to go upon
The river, he would find for her a place

'Where she could easy earn a heap of gold,'
And so, by paying him a certain sum
Each week, (which they would both agree upon;)
At last she might be free and own herself.

She clutched at the idea—and went at work
With such a ready zeal as only those
Can know who sometime in their lives have striven
For more than life or death.
      Weeks grew to years,
And each their toil and compensation brought,
And still she floated on her palace home,
Forward and fro, and sometimes stole away
To Opelousas, where her baby boy,
Though frail and delicate, was living yet.

I cannot tell you how the debt at last
Was paid—it makes another story, dears.
But fate was kind, she found a happy home
Where love's warm sunshine dried her bitter tears.
And little Phil grew up, a thoughtful lad;
I saw him at West Point not long ago
He gave me (with much hesitation, though)
A copy of a theme he wrote one day—
Only an old, old story, told in rhyme.
I'll read it, if you care to hear it now;
And that shall end my story."
    So she reads,

XIV.

LITTLE PHIL'S STORY.

[A LEGEND OF THE VIRGIN.]

THERE is an ancient legend quaint and holy,
    A story of a nun,
Who wearied of her convent life, so lowly
    Ere it was well begun.
And watching, one day, when the gate was swinging
    She fled, and ran away
Out to the wide bright world, whose voice seemed ringing
    With music all the day.

They called her Angela, this erring sister,
    So blind with discontent;
But ere from out the convent walls they missed her,
    The blessed Virgin went
And took the truant's place, and morn and even,
    With patient love and care,
Performed the tasks, late to the wanderer given;
    The penance and the prayer.

Poor nun! She found the brightness would not save her;
    The world was drear and lone;
And when she asked for bread they only gave her
    Words!—colder than a stone.
Starving, at last, she thought; starving and dying,
    Back to the convent fold
She crept, in dread despair and lowly lying,
    Begged of the Portress old,

Only a cup of water for the fever
   That burned her life away;
And when in death her eyes were closed fórever,
   That for her soul they'd pray.
The Portress hasted eager to befriend her;
   But as she passed from sight,
A woman came, with face serenely tender
   And eyes divinely bright,

And bending down with all her wondrous beauty,
   She said: "Child, do not fear;
Arise, and take again your 'customed duty,
   No one has missed you here;
See ! Am I not yourself? Not the wild maiden,
   With thoughtless, curious face,
But what you might have been in this bright aiden,
   For I have kept your place."

The blessed Virgin vanished; and the sister
   Took up the flowery cross,
Left by her shadow, where the sun had kissed her
   Upon the wall's dark moss,
And when the Portress came, no wan one lay there,
   Begging for bread and wine,
But Sister Angela pausing to pray there,
   As usual, by the shrine.

And leaving as her gift that holy token,
   The Cross, with blossoms wreathed,
As though, from every word she might have spoken,
   Some angel presence breathed.
Thus, weary mortal, when your bright hopes fail you,
   And seem to leave no trace,
Remember, they will, somewhere, yet avail you;
   Some angel keeps your place.

Immortal power is but from the immortal,
    And truth can never lie;
Soul speaks to soul, beyond form's cringing portal,
    And Love can never die.
Though we may falter from our bright ideal,
    Again, and yet again.
We always may be somewhere, strong, and real,
    Whate'er "we might have been."

    *   *   *   *   *   *

"Oh, Auntie, that is lovely," said the girls;
And tears, and smiles, and earnest, eager words
Came thick and fast as little birds in spring.
But when the comments and the chat ebbed low,
Then they turned back again to Mrs. John:
"Now, Cousin Nettie, you have no excuse;
Remember, you have promised;" but she said,
"Having been made a heroine, to-night,
An honor altogether undesired,
I think you might excuse me, for the time,
From further notoriety." But no!
They'd have a story, at whatever price,
And so she told them what she knew about
      Naming The Baby.

XV.

COUSIN NETTIE'S STORY.

[NAMING THE BABY.]

SEVEN years had we been married,
    When this wee baby-boy
Came first to claim his share of love,
    And bring his share of joy.

I remember I was sitting
    In the twilight, cool and gray,
And waiting for my husband.
    He was three weeks old, that day.

(The baby, not the husband,
    Was three weeks old, you know,)
And soon I saw him coming,
    And he kissed us, bending low.

The husband—not the baby—
    Bent and kissed us, where we sat;
And I said "This boy must have a name;
    John, what do you think of that?"

"Of course," he answered, promptly,
    "The child must have a name;
Do you know that I've been thinking,
    All day, the very same."

"Well, then, why don't you name him,"
  I asked, and he replied,
"Oh you can name him—suit yourself,
  And I'll be satisfied."

With sudden breath of fervor,
  And patriotic thrill,
I said, "Let's name him Sheridan,
  And call him Little Phil."

"Well! yes! Perhaps!" John doubtful said,
  And a frown crept in between
His quiet brows, "But then, you know,
  It makes a man feel mean

To think he's named a baby for
  Some public puppet, who,
Before the world turns over,
  May fall completely through."

Now brave-eyed keen Phil Sheridan
  Was quite my hero then,
I did not like to hear him classed
  With common public men.

However, naming baby was
  The work to do that night;
So I said, "I'd call him Willie,
  If I only thought I might."

"Pshaw! Willie! That's too common,"
  John instantly replied.
"Well, what do you think of Herman?"
  "It's rather dignified!"

"And how do you like Augustine?"
　"Augustine! That sounds weak."
"Well, Moses! There!" indignantly;
　"No, love, that's quite too meek."

"Then name him for yourself, you, John,
　I'll promise to agree;
But I'll not suggest another name;
　You find such fault with me."

"Oh don't be nervous, wifie,"
　John said, and stooped to give
The baby's face a little pinch;
　"I guess this boy will live

A few days more without a name;
　I leave it all to you;
Just please yourself with anything,
　And I'll be suited too."

Then off he went to brush his hair,
　And whistled Nellie Bly,
While I bent over baby,
　And had a little cry.

But when I spoke about a name,
　'Twas always, "Please yourself."
Until the child was three months old;
　Poor nameless little elf.

Then I was quite disgusted;
　And, so, one night I said,
While dreaming o'er my treasure,
　And fixing him for bed,

My pretty babe shall have a name
   Before this night is gone ;
Now just to plague your papa,
   I'm going to call you John.

I know it is a homely name,
   And it needs no witch to tell,
That for any sound of loving,
   I might call you *boy* as well ;

But you see 'twill make *him* angry,
   Or at least he'll be ashamed ;
And then, before you know it, sir,
   We'll have the baby named.

So then, a moment later,
   I checked a yawn to say,
" Here, husband, do take little John,
   He's been so cross to-day."

Oh what a flood of happy pride
   And tenderness and joy
Lit up that fellow's features, as
   He gazed upon his boy.

" Well ! well ! You're going to call him John,
   That's sensible, I'm sure ;
Look up here, little woman,
   What makes you so demure ?

John Jr. has a solid sound,
   And then, you know, I knew
If you would only please yourself,
   I should be suited too."

How could I crush such vanity,
 By telling him my jest?
Or hinting that his name was not
 The sweetest and the best

That ever graced a baby's brow,
 Like coronal of fame;
And after all I questioned
 Of myself, "What's in a name?"

And so I gave the matter up,
 And so the time ran on,
And so my husband thinks, I think,
 I named that baby John.
* * * * * *
Then came a laugh at Cousin John's expense,
And as it hushed, Aunt Hepsy Brown said,
 "Friends,
I haven't been invited here to speak,
But you all know I've had a checquered life."
"Oh tell us now a story, Aunty, do!
All about Phil, and how he went to sea."

So good Aunt Hepsy tells her story quaint.

XVI.

AUNT HEPZIBAH'S STORY.

[That Mr. Reporter.]

I was sitting alone, half dreaming,
    Watching the sunset pale;
Em'ly had gone with her letters
    Down to the evening mail;
When a man came up the garden,
    And opened the outer door,
And sez I—(for I thought by his actions
    He'd been that way before),

"Your name is Mr. Reporter? Eh!
    And you've just come up from town,
To find a writing woman,
    Who lives with Hepzibah Brown?
I'm getting to know your family,
    A brother of yours, I guess,
Was here last night, and a couple
    A week ago or less.

You must be doin' some business;
    For travelling expense aint small,
But it don't seem to benefit Em'ly,
    As I can see any, at all;
By the way—it's lucky for you, sir,
    That Emily's just gone out;
She wouldn't sit here a chatting,
    And wandering all about;

She'd give you one look from her big eyes,
 Steady and straight and cool,
And you'd think that a man about your size
 Was making himself a fool.
But the country is sort o' lonesome;
 And I don't object to talk;
If you think it's going to pay you
 For a ten-mile ride and walk.

In the first place, Emily Osborne,
 She's not my daughter at all;
Her father is old Squire Osborne,
 Ugly, and rich, and small.
Her mother was always feeble,
 And Emily was all she had;
No doubt she loved her fondly,
 As I loved Phil, my lad.

But when I was young and bonnie,
 The Squire came a-courtin' me;
I jilted him for a sailor,
 And that made him mad, you see;
So when my boy grew older,
 And his little pale-faced girl,
With eyes like gentian blossoms,
 And soft white hair acurl,

Begun to go, one summer,
 To the school on Munroe's hill,
That mean old varmint told her
 She was never to speak to Phil.
But twice she fell in the horse-pond,
 And Phil didn't let her drown;
And once she climbed up a cherry-tree,
 And Phil had to bring her down;

And then, when they cleared the Hart lot,
  She set her white apron afire,
And Phil wrapped her up in his overcoat,
  And kerried her home. And the Squire
Was up in the northern county;
  But his wife e'en a'most went wild,
And she kissed my boy, and blessed him,
  For savin' her darling child.

So things went on between 'em—
  I forgot how the years do fly;
They were just a couple o' babies
  To my old heart and eye—
Till one day (I was astonished)
  The *Squire* came and called on *me*—
I tried to treat him perlitely—
  And he sez, "Mrs. Brown," sez he,

"I've come here to ask you a question:
  Have you ever encouraged *your* son
To think he could marry *my* daughter?
  Just answer me that, and I've done."
Lordy Massy! That roused my temper,
  And made me most desp'rit mad.
I sez, sez I, "MR. OSBORNE,
  My Phil is his father's own lad;

Do you think he could bring his great heart,
  So noble, and strong, and true,
To think of lovin' or marryin'
  A *thing* that's related to *you?*"
The Squire gave me back an answer
  That was anything else but sweet;
And some things were said on both sides
  I don't care now to repeat.

But one thing we seemed t' agree on:
  We'd see both the children dead,
And laid out straight in their grave-clothes,
  Afore we'd *allow* 'em to wed.
That night poor Phil was moody
  And restless, and sez to me,
"Mother, how long do you think 'tis
  Since father went off to sea?"

"How long do I *think* 'tis, Philip?
  Why, he left on the tenth of May,
Two years ago come plantin'—
  I'll never forget that day."
"And where did he date his last letter?"
  "Where? Out in the China Sea;
But Philip, my boy! my baby!
  You don't think of leaving *me?*"

He went! There was no use talking!
  The baby had grown a man;
And soon I received two letters
  From the far-away coast of Japan;
One from my sailor husband,
  Full of the welcomest joy;
One with a stern-voiced courage,
  Straight from my sailor boy.

In nigh 'bout a year, my husband
  Come home! He was Captain, then;
And of all the time he was with me,
  The happiest hours were when
We talked of our brave boy Philip;
  And what he was yet to be,
And blamed Squire Osborne's daughter,
  For drivin' him off to sea.

But when the good ship *Kepler*,
    With favoring tide and wind,
Sailed out from Salem harbor,
    Her captain was left behind.
He died with his head on my shoulder;
    There was no one to comfort me;
And later came news that told me
    My Philip was lost at sea.

My heart broke then—God knows it—
    And I prayed and prayed to die.
I was stricken down with fever,
    And weary weeks went by,
In which I knew nor noontide,
    Nor night, nor dawn of day;
But the wild delirium held me,
    And I raved of my boy alway.

'Twas then that Emily found me.
    Her angry father swore
That, if once she crossed my threshold,
    She never should darken his door.
But her mother and Phil were in heaven;
    She hoped soon to meet them there;
And all for his sake she came here
    My trouble and grief to share.

And if half the strength of her lovin'
    Could be changed to silver and gold,
I never should want for comforts
    Were I twice as helpless and old.
But we have grown poor and poorer,
    And Emily stitched away
At the finest kind of 'broideries
    That didn't begin to pay.

Always a stitchin' and stitchin',
  Till the needle turned a dart,
And every time she moved it,
  I felt it in my heart.
Till at last she took to writin',
  Copying first and sich ;
And it seemed a little better
  Than the everlasting stitch.

Then her verses—there's little in 'em
  Save the moan of the sea, and Phil,
But I like to hear her read 'em,
  And they pay her, better still.
So I call my Em'ly a poet,
  But she answers shyly, "No !
Poets should be the world's teachers,
  And lead the crowds up from below,

To sunnier heights of beauty,
  Where truths like stars shine pure,
And love takes on new meanings,
  And faith in God grows sure."
So I was a dronin' and dreamin',
  While Emily's step drew near
Which me and that Mr. Reporter
  Was both too forgetful to hear.

" How long since you heard from Philip ? "
  "My Philip !" 'twas Emily's tone.
Love looks through all disguises,
  And *always claims its own.*
The days of our trouble were over,
  For there, in the twilight gray,
In the arms of that Mr. Reporter,
  My precious Emily lay.

'Twas Philip! my boy, my baby!
　　Taller than me by a head;
Bearded, and rich and handsome;
　　The sea had gi'n up its dead.
And so next day they were married,
　　When the Christmas bells rang low;
It seems like yesterday mornin',
　　Can it be 'twas a year ago?

And now we are all so happy,
　　After the care and strife,
While Emily's "bread on the waters"
　　Comes back to refresh her life.
Only I think she often
　　Wishes and longs to see
Her father, that same Squire Osborne
　　Who once came á-courting me.

　　*　　*　　*　　*　　*　　*

While we were listening to Aunt Hepsy's voice,
And while she talked, another guest came in
Unheralded, unnoticed for a time;
Until a whisper ran about the room,
And when the old dame paused, and dropped her head
In deep and silent thought, then forward strode
The late new-comer, and beside her chair
He stopped! One moment and all eyes were fixed
Upon him. Then he spoke: "I want my girl;
I want to clasp hands with my old-time friends,
And see again my parents." Then a cry
Thrilled every heart, and pretty Emily Brown
Sprang up and hung about the stranger's neck,
And sobbed, "Oh, father! father!"
　　　　　　　　　　　　　　　Grandsire spoke
With a strange, touching quiver in his voice:

"I do rejoice to bid you welcome here,
In memory of her whose gentle face
Brightened your home-life for a few brief years,
And fading, left the daughter God had sent
For you to care for. Let there be no thought
Of difference or trouble here to-night."
And wiping both his eyes he introduced
"My son! Squire Herbert Osborne."
                              Then came words
Of greeting, earnest, unequivocal,
Through which the breath of coldness faded out,
And left them friends all round.
                              Squire Osborne then
Shook hands with Philip, calling him "My son."
And now, with Emily's head still resting on
His arm, I hear him talking very low:
"Hepsy, had you been kinder, long ago,
Our lives might both have held more shine than shade;
I had not been so stern or you so sharp."
I cannot hear her answer, but I guess
The four of them will not hereafter need
More than one home!
                    There come the butternuts,
And apples and sweet cider circling round,
And Tom calls out, "Pass on the stories! you!
Whose turn comes next."
                       Of course all laugh at him
Then Cousin Nat tells of

THE "MIGHT HAVE BEEN."

Oh, a wonderful path is the "Might have been,"
    Leading up from the world's highway,
Through vales of verdure and bowers of bloom,
Through faintest breathings of sweet perfume,
    To the realms of a brighter day.

The world's highway it is weary and lone,
    But the "Might have been" path is fair ;
Fair and pleasant, and cool and wide,
With lilies leaning on either side,
    And a whisper of hope in the air.

Up that mystical, magical path I see
    A dainty white cottage, a home ;
Where a brown-haired, happy-eyed woman stands—
My wife, dear public, with outstretched hands,
    Half beckoning me to come.

And why should I mourn, that I have not dragged
    Her down to the world's highway,
To bear and share through the dust and heat,
With aching brows and faltering feet,
    The burden and toil of my day?

It is better so ! My attic nest
    May be cold, and my larder lean,
But "my wife," "our children," each precious word,
With a loving echo is faintly heard
    From the heights of the "Might have been."

So I walk and work on the world's highway
    Content that in God's good time
I shall know why the radiant
    "Might have been,"
That came so near to my eager ken
    Was not, and is not mine.

*   *   *   *   *   *

He is a poet, is our cousin Nat,
His rhymes are floating everywhere, and when
They call upon his father, Uncle Nat,
To add his story to the storied eve,
We'll find it ready written. Here it is:

XVII.

UNCLE NAT'S STORY.

[THREESCORE YEARS.]

THE year was dying in the night,
　The bells were ringing loud and clear;
The snow upon the earth lay white,
　As a bride upon her bier;

And as the Old Year slipped away,
　Solemn and silent, sad and slow,
A mother found her New Year's gift,
　Just threescore years ago.

Oh, mother heart, o'erflowing then
　With hope and blessing, saddest joy;
What unknown future could you ken,
　For that wee baby boy?

Ah, how you prayed that God would guard
　The changeful paths those feet must go—
Fair dimpled feet on life's rough road,
　Just threescore years ago.

But babyhood in childhood merged,
　And childhood sprang to manhood fleet;
The city set its wildering snares
　To catch those untried feet;

Then wide and bright the prairie land—
    The Eldorado of the West,
Called him from all the household band
    For newer home in quest.

And full of faith and hope he went,
    Ready to battle fate or foe ;
With youth and health his only wealth,
    Just twoscore years ago.

But soon a radiant star appeared
    On the horizon of his life,
The future new importance wore,
    He won a lovely wife.

Oh, blessing of all blessings best,
    Companion, helpmate, faithful heart ;
Whom God hath joined forevermore
    No power on earth can part.

Then time ran on in happy tides ;
    Years came, and went, and brought their share
Of busy labor and reward,
    Of household love and care.

And first a blossom of a girl
    Beside the quiet hearthstone grew,
And later, and as welcome quite,
    A bright-eyed boy came too.

The children grew to youth in turn,
    And bright the fire of love did glow ;
Naught could be happier than that home
    A score of years ago.

But the mother's health was failing then :
   Slowly but surely, day by day,
As fade the leaves in autumn time,
   Her slight strength ebbed away.

Her step grew light, her breath grew short,
   And yet she kept her wonted place,
No sorrow in her loving heart,
   No shadow on her face.

And he, the husband of her youth,
   Watched her with tenderest patience ever ;
He bore her in his strong fond arms
   Close to the shining river.

She only fell asleep, one night,
   Her head upon his shoulder lying ;
So gently came the messenger,
   We did not think her dying.

But in the bright eternal world,
   Escaped from every care below,
She woke to angel life, just half
   A score of years ago.

And loneliness with sorrow came.
   He missed the dear familiar face,
The presence of the fragile form
   From its accustomed place.

And half in doubt and half in hopes
   His weary aching heart to fill,
He tried to rear another shrine
   Beside his hearthstone still.

He tried and failed. The shrine would fall
  In dust and ashes. And his life,
Though true and upright, frank and free,
  Was darkened by the strife.

But as the ship outrides the storm,
  And sturdy oak defies the blast,
So did his honest pride return
  Triumphantly at last.

And now from every shackle free,
  Slow drifting toward life's sunset hour,
He knows his loved wife waits for him
  Upon the shining shore;

For often, when the twilight comes,
  He seems to hear her loving tone,
And almost feel her gentle hand
  Reach down to clasp his own.

And all his friends—he has no foes—
  Unite to wish him hearty cheer,
And hope his life may yet be spared
  Another score of years.

* * * * * *

Then Tom slow looking round the happy group,
Spies Uncle Christopher! "Now, now, old friend,
Don't you be backward in this forward cause;
Trot out and show your paces; let us hear,
Some theme from your capacious knowledge-box."
"Oh, stop your blarney," answers Uncle Chris,
"I'll tell a story half a mile in length,
If but to hush the music of your voice."
          And so he tells

XVIII.

UNCLE CHRISTOPHER'S STORY.

[AMONG THE MINES.]

'TWAS out in California,
　In the days of Forty-nine,
When every hill was thought to hold
　The richest kind of a mine,
That I first saw Minnie Martin;
　She was sweet and winsome then,
But she never would have chosen me,
　From forty other men,

Save for a strange adventure;
　It makes my blood run cold,
To think of it, and you, I'm sure,
　Would faint to hear it told!
"Now Christopher,"—Aunt Minnie's face,
　Puts on a pleading air—
"Why will you tease the children so?
　I don't think you are fair!"

"But wifey you are always fair,"
　Says jolly Uncle Kit,
"Two fair ones in one family
　Would be overdoing it.
So I guess I'll tell the story,
　Unvarnished, plain, and true;
And leave the fancy 'bellishments
　And fixing up to you.

Squire Martin left this little town
   When Minnie was eighteen,
He was California-fever struck,
   And he had it awful mean.
What makes you look so wondering, boys?
   You don't know what that is?
Ah well! Thank God you never will,
   For now it's a played-out biz.

But he took his wife and daughter,
   When he went with the Forty-niners,
And struck right out prospecting,
   With a lot of hardy miners;
He tried to leave the women,
   In 'Frisco, down by the bay;
But they grew desperate homesick
   Without him, and would not stay.

So up they came to the mountains,
   To the roughest kind of a camp·
You ever clapped your eyes on—
   One of the "first-class" stamp;
I can't begin to describe it;
   Though some of the miners' wives
Were there, and they rather brightened
   Our wild, romantic lives.

The Squire had another cabin,
   Put up as soon as he could;
His wife was bound to like it,
   And called it neat and good.
But a pretty girl like Minnie
   Was a rarity there just then,
And we almost looked upon her
   As a Saint. We rugged men.

One night we planned a picnic,
   And knocked off work for a day,
We wanted to visit " Jessie Peak,"
   A couple o' miles away.
We took our rifles with us,
   Our dogs, and a bugle-call,
And we made quite a merry party—
   A dozen, I reckon, in all.

Now here comes in the romance, boys ;
   I wonder if 'twill do
To waste an hour this evening
   In telling it to you ?
It might set you off hunting,
   For caverns black as night,
To play " Babes of the woods" in,
   And give your friends a fright.

We climbed the peak, however,
   And planted a flagstaff there,
From which the glorious Stars and Stripes
   Swung out on the cool bright air.
We filled our hands with specimens,
   Our pockets full of rocks,
And our brains with glowing visions
   Of future mining stocks.

We ate our simple dinner
   With fruits—oh ! such a feast
As nature never offered
   In the old time home " Down East,"
And then we started camp-ward
   With loitering footsteps slow,
Discussing rather carelessly
   The nearest way to go.

I watched with jealous interest
  To keep by Minnie's side,
And talked about the prospect
  Before us spreading wide.
I picked the finest geodes
  From their rocky river-bed,
And pointed out the fleecy clouds
  Slow sailing overhead.

And so, by some contrivin',
  I let the party stray
Just out of sight, while she and I
  Went dreaming on our way;
Then we took to hunting gulches,
  And soon to exploring "leads,"
And finally we thrust aside
  The underbrush and weeds,

And crept with bended heads inside
  A funny little cave,
When down came loosened earth and stone;
  'Twas darker than a grave.
We both were stunned and breathless,
  And first thought we were killed,
But when the dust had settled
  That our eyes and nostrils filled,

Then we began to breathe again,
  And found ourselves all right,
But hidden in a darker tomb
  Than old Egyptian night.
We shouted, but our voices
  Were lost in hollow space,
My arm still clung to Minnie,
  Though I could not see her face.

She would not let me leave her
  To explore our prison cell,
So we clambered round together
  For awhile, and then stood still,
Hopeless! though saying nothing
  About it, and I tried
All trace of fear or doubting
  From my trembling voice to hide.

So brave and calm was Minnie,
  In her own quiet way,
It made me hate myself, boys,
  For leading her astray.
If I'd been alone, I reckon,
  I'd a tried to burrow through;
But I couldn't risk her life, boys,
  And I didn't know what to do.

The rocks were loose and shaky,
  The roof was very low,
I had no tools for digging,
  And I darsn't strike a blow.
I never felt so wretched
  Before, since I was born;
And Minnie's patient courage
  Just made me more forlorn.

I had a little basket
  Of berries in my hand;
They'd keep her from starvation,
  Two days or so, I planned.
In less than that time, surely,
  Some help would set us free,
But every chance of danger
  Was a bitter scourge to me.

She asked me would her father
    Go on and leave us here?
"Perhaps he might," I answered,
    Because the night was near,
And he knew the mountain gulches
    Were dangerous and deep,
Where the moonlight could not reach them,
    And the shadows lay asleep.

But we were safely hidden
    In our funny little nest;
I tried to laugh, and treat it
    As though it was a jest.
Then I measured out her supper,
    And when she'd eaten that,
I fixed her a place for sleeping,
    A sort of leafy mat.

And I sat down beside her;
    I didn't sleep a wink;
And she, though very quiet,
    Was wakeful too, I think.
At last I thought 'twas morning,
    She stirred and seemed to rise;
Oh, what would I ha' given,
    For a look at her two eyes.

But soon we had our breakfast;
    She made me eat some then,
And we talked about explorin'
    Our hiding-place again.
The hours were long and silent,
    But when I thought 'twas noon,
I didn't like to tell her,
    The day would pass so soon.

So I says, "I guess you'd better,
   Eat some luncheon, Minnie, dear."
Says she, " I don't feel hungry ;
   Will father soon be here?"
Just then I heard a scratching,
   A quick and eager whine ;
I knew my old dog Hero's voice
   As well as he knew mine.

Then strong hands moved the rubbish,
   The glad light filtered through,
And we crept out in safety
   'Neath Heaven's own arch of blue.
Squire Martin clasped his daughter,
   And breathed a silent prayer ;
While I looked round bewildered,
   Upon the party there.

The sun was settin' slowly,
   The clouds all gold and flame ;
The boys and dogs and baskets
   All seemed the very same.
How long do you think we'd been there,
   In that cavern dark and still ?
Two hours and twenty minutes,
   By the best watch on the hill.

We didn't breathe a whisper
   About that long, long night,
But we seemed to belong to each other,
   By some mysterious right.
And so I stuck to Minnie
   As though I'd saved her life ;
And how about the wedding?
   Well, now—you'll tell 'em, wife.

UNCLE CHRISTOPHER'S STORY.

*   *   *   *   *   *

"There isn't much to tell," Aunt Minnie says,
For father right away gave his consent.
I wore a cotton gown, and—"
                         "There's a sleigh!"
Call out a score of voices ringing loud,
And ears and eyes are soon all busy with
A new arrival.   Strangely opportune
It seems.   'Tis Uncle Christopher's one boy,
His Lawrence, and straight to his mother's arms
The youngster goes without a backward look,
As a hen-brooded duckling to the brook.
Aunt Prue has gathered closely to her side
A slender, childish figure, and they two
Have disappeared unnoticed.
                           But the boy
Is being kissed and cuddled, passed about,
His two hands shaken and his bright hair pulled,
As though they all forgot that he had grown
A stalwart fellow.   Till at last he stands
Laughing and blushing by his mother's chair,
Waiting a chance to tell his story o'er
And hear her answer.   Still he does not tell
How he's been hiding for the last four days
Down at the village inn, protected by
Aunt Prudence and our own brave Cousin Tom;
But listen to his pleading voice.   He tells

XIX.

COUSIN LAWRENCE'S STORY.

[THE CHRISTMAS GIFT.]

Home again! Home again! Mother, dear,
Pleasantest words for a man to hear:
Your boy, you call me, your brave boy still;
Ah, mother, mine, I have wandered long,
    And, as wanderers will,
Have learned, perhaps, less good than ill.
But list, while I tell you, half story, half song,
Where I've been, what I've done; judge me then, right or wrong.

I had been lapped in San Anguile
All summer long, where the winds blow cool,
Regaining the health I lost at school,
And losing the slight and hacking cough,
For which you remember you sent me off,
To that magical sea-swept isle.

And there I found a birdie brown,
A shy, wild sparrow, with soft, bright eyes;
'Twould have filled me then with a queer surprise,
If that birdie brown had fluttered down,
And begged to rest on my grausome breast
    For even a little while.

But I snared and tempted the fluttering thing,
And all unwittingly clipped its wing,
'Till it did not try to soar or sing,

But left the mountains free and blue
To follow wherever I might roam,
And so, dear mother, I brought it home,
    As a Christmas gift to you.

And there I found a Mexic maid,
With soft, black hair in shining braid,
    And eyes like a wild gazelle;
She came with milk from the ranche hard by,
And fruits from God's great vineyard near;
I watched her ways with a curious eye,
    More close than I like to tell.
And often and often I saw her peer
At the books and papers lying about;
Sometimes she would smile almost in fear,
And sometimes timidly reaching out
Her small brown hand, she would touch with awe
The mystical printed page she saw.

'Till it minded me, in a dreamy way,
(As low in my wind-rocked hammock I swung,
And watched the oriole as she hung
Her tinier hammock with daintier sway,
    Far up 'mong the leaves at play;)
It minded me as a kindly deed,
That perhaps I might teach the child to read,
    So I 'gan my lessons that very day.

She was apt and merry, and loved to learn;
Her cheek would flush and her dark eye burn
When I talked of our northern ladies fair;
Her father, it seems, was a northman too,
But her mother was Spanish through and through.
Both had passed from this world of care,
Leaving, with all her beauty rare,

This bright little waif, so strangely allied,—
Northern ambition and Southern pride.

At last I knew I must say farewell
To my idle life, and that sea-swept isle,
To the dreamy languor of San Anguile,
    And I told the Mexic maiden so.
Never a tear from her bright eyes fell,
But a look of helpless and hopeless woe
Crept and quivered about her lips,
And shadowed her face with its strange eclipse,
Until I knew, by her troubled looks—
She did not like to give up her books.

But she stitched me a belt with her fingers deft,
Such as the traders wear, to hold
Safely hidden their store of gold;
And she tossed me a light "good-by," as I left.
Low on the beach I saw her stand,
Shading her eyes with her slender hand.
I was almost sorry to leave her there;
But the tide was up and the wind was fair,
And off I went to the rough mainland.

Thence to the town whence the coach would start,
    Where I lingered a week or more,
Loth from that pleasant place to part,
    And wishing my journey o'er.
But launched at last on the lonely road,
    Slowly climbing the mountain side,
Soon we left all trace of human abode;
    I shall never forget that ride.
Two rough boys from some mining camp,
    Two tall Mexicans, evil-eyed,
And one who belonged to neither stamp,

A small, dark man, in a slouching hat,
Who still as death in his corner sat.

The miners slept as night drew near;
The Mexicans chatted and grumbled and laughed,
And many a draught of liquor quaffed,
　　Which I only half refused to share,
'Till one to the other, leering, spoke,
"Suppose we go outside for a smoke."
And they tossed me a flask, and said, "Drink deep,
Comrade, 'tis good. 'Twill help you sleep."
I heard the fall of their heavy feet,
As they slowly climbed to the driver's seat;
Then I poured from the flask a brimming cup,
And smiling thoughtfully, held it up.

The small, dark man, with the slouching hat,
Sprang out of the corner where he sat,
Sprang out with a quick and stealthy bound,
And striking the cup and turning it o'er,
And spilling the liquid along the floor,
Said, hoarsely whispering, " Drink no more!
The stuff is drugged." I turned around.
The man in the corner silent crouched,
And lower his hat o'er his forehead slouched.
The miners slept in the fitful gleam—
I thought for a moment 'twas all a dream—
That my vision blurred, and the red wine spilled.
So again the cup from the flask I filled,
And raised it slowly. That voice again
Shrieked low in my ear, as if in pain,
Saying, " The stuff is drugged, I swear,
And little those black-browed villains care.

If you never wake, so they share and share
The gold that is stitched in the belt you wear."

My life was saved, for I drank no more,
Nor slept; and the rangers muttered and swore;
But I wondered much why that man should guess,
I'd a golden belt 'neath my plain coarse dress.

Far up on the mountains a storm came down,
Fierce and sudden, and sharp and swift;
The coach stuck fast in a monstrous drift,
    Twenty good miles from town.
In vain we struggled to dig her out;
The fine flakes eddied and swirled about,
'Till, at last, the driver, all wearied out,
    Unhitched the horses and started off,
Ploughing his way through the cruel sleet;
And the miners ploughed after that driver, Jem,
And the evil-eyed Mexicans ploughed after them.
But I could not drag my freezing feet
    Through the treacherous snow, so soft.

I was tired and sleepy, and longed to rest,
E'en there on the cold white mountain's breast;
So, sinking slowly, I dreamed of you;
'Till a whisper came on the wings of the storm,
And something thrilled my pulses through;
The summery breath of San Anguile,
Or the music of dreamland's haunted isle,
Was never so sweet and warm.

I woke! The man with the slouching hat
Deep in the drift beside me sat,
His arm about me, his clinging lips
Sending the blood to my finger tips.

Mother—that man—was—my girlie dear.
She had followed me from the sea-swept shore,
And saved my poor life, o'er and o'er;
I could not freeze with her so near,
And—she is the sparrow shy and swift,
I brought you home for a Christmas gift.

Mother—thank Heaven I see you smile,
Did you guess what was coming, all the while?
  But, oh! forgive me, do!
And kiss, for my sake, my Mexic maid;
Ah, mother, dear, I was half afraid—
  But she is so fond and true.
   * * * * * *
Then brave Aunt Margaret came forward, with
Her arm twined close about the Mexic maid.
(Aunt Prue was crying so she could not speak)
And every one seemed to forget to be
Angry, or even sorry, when they saw
The look of deep ineffable content,
That filled, at least, two pairs of loving eyes,
And brightened all the others.
        Listen now,
As Cousin Kate from somewhere brings to light
A little book of sweet imperfect rhymes,
Written by Emily Osborne.
        And she reads,
In her soft, low-toned, sympathetic voice:

XX.

COUSIN KATE'S STORY.

[LEGEND OF THE WALTZES.]

IN a gray, old, Austrian tower,
At the mystic twilight hour,
Sat a youth and maiden, dreaming,
    Watching down the setting sun;
While around them, rising, swelling,
Came the vesper music, telling
That another twelve hours' labor
    In the world below was done.

Suddenly, athwart their dreaming,
Broke a sound of harsher meaning,
And the Royal Princess, summoned
    From her teacher, bade farewell
To the twilight and the tower,
And the passion-freighted hour,
And the lesson love had taught her
    In the music's echoing swell.

And the youth, alone and lonely,
Saw a radiant vision only,
Saw two violet eyes that lighted
    All the spaces, dusk and dim,
Heard above the music's swelling,
Something to his spirit telling
That his own heart's treasure waited
    With a loyal faith for him.

But through castle, court, and garden,
Rang the voice of groom and warden—
"Ope' the great portcullis! Open!
    For the Earl is drawing near;"
And far up the winding stair,
Came the bidding to prepare
Music for the coming bridal
    Of the Princess, sweet Sophia.

Heavy heart and brow of sorrow
Could not stay the coming morrow,
Could not give the young musician
    Freedom from the King's command.
So he wrought, with varying feeling,
Pride and grief and anger stealing
Through the sounding chords that echoed
    From his busy brain and hand.

Once again, at twilight hour,
Pealed the bells from dome and tower,
As the glittering bridal party swept
    Within the castle keep.
Bright the banquet hall was glowing,
Red the wine cups gleamed, o'erflowing,
Pale the bride was, as a lily, in the
    Moonlight hushed to sleep.

But at midnight, weird and eerie,
Summoned from his Donjon eyrie,
Came the wondrous young musician,
    Graver far than e'er before.
And the guests made way before him,
And the banners fluttered o'er him,
And the harpers tuned their viols,
    And the waltzers beat the floor.

Hush! A breath of music thrilling
Every pulse a moment stilling,
Stole across the mute assemblage—
  'Rose, and soared, and sank, and died.
Then a ripple stirred the measure,
Like a sigh of wordless pleasure,
And a low exultant murmur
  Thridded the melodious tide.

Then a sweet harmonious rolling;
Were the vesper-bells slow tolling?
Were the little children singing,
  Or the sad-voiced nuns at prayer?
Nay! 'twas but the midnight dirges
Of the ocean's solemn surges,
Breaking on the lonely beaches
  With an echo of despair.

Still the waltzers circled fleeter,
And the music clearer, sweeter,
Held them like a tropic serpent,
  With its wizard coil and fold,
Till the light feet lagged more slowly,
And some fell, and fainted, wholly,
And some left the witching circle
  Pale and breathless, still and cold.

Yet the melody clomb higher
On its wings of liquid fire,
Guided by the young composer,
  Swaying slowly, left and right,
Watching but his own heart's treasure
Floating through the dreamy measure,
With her smiling lips half parted,
  And her radiant eyes alight.

Not a word by either spoken
Told that two fond hearts were broken;
Not a flush of rose or crimson
    On the bride's pale bosom slept.
Every eye was fixed unaltering,
But the music, never faltering,
Held its strange, remorseless power,
    While the viols wailed and wept.

Suddenly, her hands outreaching,
As with passionate prayer, beseeching
Her young lover not to leave her;
    His dear name she murmured o'er;
"Strauss, mein Strauss." Her soul had risen
From its frail but beauteous prison,
And, borne upward on the music,
    She was his forevermore.

*   *   *   *   *   *

We praise the poem, never questioning
If the sad story be or true or false.
And now we turn to Cousin Kate for "more;"
She gives the book to Emily, saying, "Here;
No one can know so well as your dear self
The spirit of these words. Please read to us."
And Emily, turning o'er the written leaves,
Says, "Here I find a mere schoolgirlish theme,
All bright with imagery. Some traveller
Has told me that he saw in Italy
A small, dark ruin of a darker age,
Now called the Vestal Temple.
                              But I think
My own description far outrivals his;
And so if one would not have anything

To disappoint one, let him stay at home,
And draw upon his own imaginings
For foreign scenes."
    " But if," says Cousin Tom,
" One has no bright imaginative store ;
What then ?"
    "Ah, then," laughs Emily in reply,
" Lacking the power to build such temples fair,
Why, one must needs endure the long fatigue
Of travel and sea-sickness, but to find
How poor is any ancient ruined pile
Compared with pictures conjured in the brain ;
However, if you'll listen, I will read."

XXI.

COUSIN EMILY'S STORY.

[THE TEMPLE OF VESTA.]

By the side of the River of Roses,
  That flows from the Apennine hills,
On its way to the blue Adriatic,
  With a murmur that time never stills,
There once stood the Temple of Vesta,
  The temple to fire consecrate;
And fire was the synonym sacred
  Of mystery, life, light, and fate.

This temple was builded of marble,
  Its dome like a mound of pure snow,
Its corner-stone carven in jasper,
  Its foundations of porphyry below.
It had portals of sard and sardonyx,
  With arches of malachite green,
And pillars of columnar crystal,
  With pavings of agate between.

There were Altars—three altars—where always
  The quenchless fires burned, day and night,
And each altar was shaped pentahedral—
  One blue, and one green, and one white.
There first was the Altar of Effort,
  The Altar of learning and youth,
All fashioned of deep-tinted Sapphire,
  Symbolic of friendship and truth.

And second, the Altar of Action,
   Of knowledge by effort acquired,
Was builded of pale-tinted beryl,
   Symbolic of labor inspired.
And third was the Altar Fruition,
   The Altar of teaching so fair,
Carved quaintly from pure alabaster,
   Symbolic of guidance and care.

And every seven years there were chosen,
   From royalest households in Rome,
Four maidens, mere seven-summered children,
   The blessing and sunshine of home.
For three times seven years, they were chosen
   To plenish the Vestaline fires,
And under the vow of the priestess,
   They banished all human desires.

With reverent heads bowed, and hands folded
   Half proudly, and yet half in awe,
They promised the holiest allegiance
   And faith, to the Vestaline law.
Young creatures, they scarce comprehended
   The mystical goal to be won,
In their long years of self-abnegation
   That numbered just one score and one.

In which they were never to falter,
   Or shrink from their tasks day or night,
But to fuel the flames on the altars,
   To keep them, as beacon-fires bright.
To garland the temple with blossoms,
   To purify chancel and nave,
And to guard from all stain or dishonor,
   Each corridor, pillar and pave.

But the hand of the priestess of Vesta,
   Hand of man must not clasp it, or press,
And the heart of the priestess of Vesta
   Must not thrill at love's kiss or caress.
So in that far-off age, half forgotten,
   As seen through time's mystical night,
They wrought in the Temple of Vesta,
   Twelve maidens, all virginal white,

Were their garments, with girdles of lilies,
   And sandals of ivory fair,
And helmets of pure beaten silver,
   And fillets of pearls for their hair?
These maidens, the virgins of Vesta,
   Had each her own work, and her shrine,
Where travellers knelt to do homage,
   Where the famished were nourished with wine,

Where torches burned out or extinguished
   Were kindled, and lighted anew,
Where eyes that saw only the false light
   Were opened, at last, to the true.
Where the weary found rest, and were cared for,
   The erring were taught, and forgiven,
The lost and benighted were guided,
   And *all* pointed upward to Heaven.

Round the altar of Effort were clustered
   Brave, bright little hearts, strong and pure.
They feared not, alas! for they knew not,
   What they yet might be called to endure.
They were Learners, and all looking forward
   To futures of usefulness rare;
Joy, Innocence, Trust, and Devotion,
   Were the names that were given them there.

Rose-tinted of quartz and cornelian,
    Gold paved, with no hint of alloy,
And echoing with music and laughter,
    Was the shrine of the virgin of Joy;
In a shrine made from pearl and white onyx,
    Untarnished by metal or clay,
And pure as the moonbeams at midnight,
    The virgin of Innocence lay.

Like a couch in the great rock of ages,
    Safe hidden from mildew and rust,
And cushioned and pillowed with eider,
    Was the shrine of the virgin of Trust.
The shrine of the virgin Devotion
    Was fashioned of Chrysoprase rare,
Its echoless portals were silent,
    Made sacred to worship and prayer.

By the Altar of Labor, of Action,
    The Workers, self-centred and true,
Pride, Faith, Hope, and Patience, were gathered,
    Each ready to dare and to do;
Nor forward, nor backward, their eyes turned,
    Enough for the day was the task,
And for future result or rewarding
    The *workers* paused never to ask.

Like a fortress impregnably guarded,
    That a myriad shocks had defied,
All builded of granite and iron,
    Was the shrine of the virgin of Pride.
The shrine of the virgin of Faith, rose
    A tower of strength for the weak,
And opened its Amethyst portals
    With shelter, for all who might seek.

The shrine of the virgin of Hope glowed
    With the tints of the rainbow at even,
The pale, changeful, flame-hearted Opal,
    To her tireless keeping was given.
The shrine of the virgin of Patience
    Was builded, and fashioned of thorns
She had taken from brows that were bleeding,
    And hearts that were weary and torn.

By the radiant altar Fruition,
    The Teachers so gentle and wise,
Look back on their work well accomplished,
    With love in their beautiful eyes.
They were Memory, Mercy, and Power,
    With Charity, greatest of all,
And they felt that as guides of the children,
    They never must falter or fall.

There, touched with the faint loving glamour
    Of backward bewitching old time,
With hints that no future could brighten,
    Stood Memory's crystalline shrine;
The shrine of the virgin of Mercy
    Was builded of Jacinth, and crowned
With a prayer from a young heart made happy,
    That lonely and sad she had found.

The shrine of the virgin of Power,
    The virgin whom mortals call Might,
Was builded of Jasper, with pillars
    Of rubies and emeralds bright.
But Charity, blessedest virgin,
    Little recked how her shrine might be wrought,
So its portals admitted each wanderer
    And gave to them *all* some kind thought.

We travellers on Life's weary highway,
  Slow wandering by time's mystic stream,
We know that the temple of Vesta
  Is not all a fable, a dream.
We have striven at the altar of Effort,
  At the altar of Action have wrought,
And knelt at the altar Fruition,
  Perhaps not in life, but in thought.

And sometimes when storm clouds have gathered,
  And wrapped us in terror and doubt,
And fear lights her Will O'Wisp lantern,
  And tauntingly swings it about,
Benighted, and heart-sick, and weary,
  We falter on, ready to fall,
Then far off the Temple lights shining,
  Proclaim "There is rest here for all."
*   *   *   *   *   *
"And here," continued Emily, "is a bit
Of rhyme I wrote, intending to compare
Our Odin to that mythical old god,
The Odin of the Scandinavians,
Whose picture haunts our public now and then."

ODIN.

Symbol of all might and power
  Was the War God of the North;
Fearing naught, and all defying,
  Leading his great armies forth
From each mountain gorge and fastness;
  From Valhalla's silent halls,
Came the troops and hordes of Odin,
  Answering dumbly to his call.

In his hand a spear he carried,
    On his feet he sandals wore ;
And the mantle wrapped about him
    Was a storm-cloud dark and hoar ;
Near him sailed a snowy petrel
    Telling him when hope was bright ;
At his side a raven fluttered,
    Memory, strange and dark as night.

And when forth he stróde to battle,
    At his feet twin wolves crouched back ;
Geri, the subduer, snow white ;
    Fenri, the destroyer, black.
Thus the mighty War God Odin,
    Type of strength and earnest thought,
Ever to his myriad subjects
    Some new·scheme for conquering taught.

But our gentler age and culture
    Old time types hath cast away,
And the strength of worth and wisdom
    Marks the Odin of to-day.
Firm as patient—wise as loving,
    Strong warm hands and brave true heart,
In the world of care and trouble
    Ready still to bear his part ;

In his merry fashion scorning
    All our paltry pride of birth,
Counting fame an idle bauble,
    Gold and gear as little worth ;
Yet we know, where'er he wanders,
    Deeds of kindness mark his way,
And the charm of true affection
    Guards the Odin of to-day.

* * * * * *

Now once again the tide of talk ebbs low,
And through the driving storm we hear a sound
Of sleigh-bells! In an instant every eye
Lights up with hope, and every eager face
Turns toward the door; but hope and eagerness
Fade slowly in a dumb, bewildered stare;
There stand two muffled figures in our midst;
The snow is shining on their garments dark,
And dripping slowly on the sanded floor.
Grandma goes forward first, and reaches out
Her trembling hands, and says, "My little girl."
And Helen Winthrop drops the heavy wraps
That cling about her, and her wan, white face
And large dark eyes look weird and sorrowful.
Her father stands beside her; all his pride
Subdued into a gentle dignity.
"My friends," he says, "day after day I've seen
My daughter, whose bright eyes and ruddy bloom
Were once the joy and glory of my life,
Fading as fade the flowers in Autumn time;
She made no moan, she uttered no complaint.
But since her friend, your kinsman, Odin Pratt
Left us so suddenly, alas! alas!
The sunshine from my home has vanished with
The merry music from her ringing laugh.
I blame myself, no doubt you blame me too,
But will you not believe me when I say
I knew not what I did? The demon pride
Possessed me; and my one and only thought
Was, 'Here is mine old enemy at last
By representative placed in my power,
Now will I glut mine ire, and punish him;'
I am ashamed for the harsh, foolish words,

My temper made me speak ; I knew no harm
Of the young man, nor had I ever heard
A breath to his discredit, and for weeks
After he went away, I had no thought
That his departure could have aught to do
With Helen's listless manner : but I asked,
' Why do you stay so much at home, my dear ?
What keeps you watching at the window-pane
All day, and, too, for aught I know, all night.'
' Father, I wait for Odin Pratt,' she said :
A flood of anger swept across my soul ;
But when she raised her pleading, wistful eyes,
Although the words I spoke were cold and stern,
My heart ached for her. Weary weeks have passed
Since then, in which our lives have struggled on
Hopeless and bitter : but this morn I heard
Down at the village that you had received
Late news from Odin. Not a word I spake
At home concerning this, but long ere night
Some prating tongue told Helen he was dead ;
That tidings had been brought from Washington,
Telling you when and where he passed from earth.
Then (looking at my daughter's pallid face)
I said, ' I'll send a servant to inquire
If this report be true.'

       ' I cannot trust
A servant,' she replied. ' But I will ask
That they shall send the letter straight to you.'
Then her eyes blazed ! ' And think you they will send
The record of their anguish and their grief
To you who caused it ? ' And she covered up
Her tense, calm face, with her white wasted hands,
And moaned, but wept not.

Long, slow hours crept by;
I sat alone and watched the study fire,
And Helen took her place again beside
The western window. Suddenly her voice
Rang sharp and wofully. 'Oh, father, see;
The lights are flitting swiftly round the house
At Grandsire Pratt's! I see a crowd of men!
Something has happened—Father! take me there.'
I tried to reason with her; useless task!
Her sensitive, unreasoning, woman's heart,
That ne'er asserted its weak self before,
Now plead and called, and would not be repressed.
'Oh, father, let me go to Grandma Pratt.
Aunt Prudence loves me, she will care for me,
And if they've brought my Odin home to-night—
Oh, father, take me—' A quick, gasping sob
Told me more plainly than her broken words
That something must be done! And so! and so—"

The tall, strong man looks round and hesitates.
Helen is nestled 'mong white pillows deep,
Between Aunt Prue and Grandma, and a smile
Flits round her quivering mouth, and lights her eyes
Like moonlight, 'mong the shadows. At her feet
Are Nan, and Kate, and Bessie looking up
With happy faces, to her happy face,
While just behind her chair stands merry Tom
And graceful Cousin Nat.
                         A dozen more
Are hov'ring round her like a swarm of bees
About a clover blossom. Uncle King
Is talking with Judge Winthrop, fast and low;
They both look pleased and earnest.

Grandsire stands
Between them, speaking little, feeling much.
And now Squire Osborne goes to join their talk,
And Uncle 'Liab follows Uncle Luke.
'Tis hard for them to give a welcoming hand
To one whom they have made a point to slight
For many years,—but he has swallowed first
The bitter pill of pride, and taken first
A step toward reconciliation true.
And so they talk till Tom creeps slyly round
And says, " Tell us a story, Grandma, do,
You haven't told us one to-night, you know."
Aunt Prudence laughs. " Will your insatiate greed
For stories never cease?" But Grandma says:
"No, children, we must stop our chatter now,
It is not like that any one can come
From any distance in this driving storm,
The night wanes late. You have already had
Too much excitement. Let us now compose
Our minds, and so make ready for the hour
Of family worship. Helen, love, draw up
The shawl about your shoulders; Bessie dear,
Give her that hassock, lest her feet are damp."
But Helen's father says: " Daughter, you've had
A draught from some Elysian spring, I think.
Now let us homeward hie with happy hearts."

"Not in this storm," a dozen voices cry:
" Oh stay with us; we've room enough, for all
The horses in their stalls are safely housed,
And Pat and Pete, with old Bartholomew,
Are roasting apples, filling cider mugs,
And finding comfort in the servants' room."
Judge Winthrop shakes his head. " It will not do;

I am a happier man for coming here,
And Helen is, I know, a happier girl,
But we must not intrude upon your joy.
Let's have one hymn, and then we'll say 'Good-night.'"

A few words more, and then the hymn-books come,
Brought from their shelf beside the oaken desk,
And scattered liberally among the guests.
Now Grandma finds a favorite hymn, and says
"You all can sing this! Let the tune be that
To which the old One Hundredth psalm is set."
And now the choral rises, grandly sweet.

HYMN.

Father of all, Thy care we bless,
Which crowns our families with peace;
From Thee they spring and by Thy hand
They have been and are still sustained.

To God, most worthy to be praised,
Be our domestic altars raised;
He bids the noisy tempest cease;
He calms the raging seas to peace.

Oh may each future age proclaim
The honors of Thy glorious name,
While pleased and thankful we remove
To join the family above.
                                        DODDRIDGE.

The hymn is hushed! each reverent head bends low,
And every heart is heavy with Amen!
When! Hark! A tramp of hoofs, a sound of bells,
A shout of merry voices strong and deep;
A dozen reaching hands fling wide the door;
A score of feet rush out into the night;

The storm has ceased, the moon is looking forth,
And by her radiant lustre all can see
A pair of prancing horses and a sleigh
Holding three figures—there are surely three—
Now rings a shout from the approaching team.
"'Tis Odin's voice!" " Odin is coming home!"
" Our Odin!   God be praised!" " Hurrah! Hurrah!"
Oh babble of interminable tongues!
But who comes with him?
                        They are at the door.
Pat takes the horses! they all three come in,
Odin—and the two strangers,—can it be—
(See them kiss Grandma)—yes, 'tis Uncle Tom
And—Eric,—for he greets Aunt Prudence next,
And standing by her, hear him introduce
To her, perhaps more than the rest,
                               " My son
Eric Fitz Eric Fitz Ericsen, friends."
Odin—our Odin with that sounding name.

Now Eric tells, in rapid broken words,
About the old-time trouble, coming when
Christiania was blockaded in the south
And Trondjean barricaded in the north.
" I could not leave my Norman fastness then
(And all our sturdy honest country folk),
Knowing my father had such need of me ;
And so I thought to send my child to you
After his mother died.   Thomas was there ;
He volunteered to pass the enemy's lines
(' Run the blockade' I think you call it here.)
For this we had the documents made out,
T' establish his identity, and writ
On clearest parchment, in good English, too,

As well as in our Scandinavian text;
And father blessed the sturdy little waif,
And gave him to an honest sailor's care,
After he lisped for one last time his prayer
And the old mythologic nursery rhyme,
To Odin, for deliverance and success.
But they were followed, and the ship we sent
Was boarded by the enemy, and sunk.
Thomas was taken prisoner, and the child
Vanished as vanishes a flake of snow
The sun shines on.
     Of course, news soon came back
Of the lost ship, and, after many days,
Thomas was ransomed, and returned to me.
And, later, when we took the very ship
That captured ours, we found among her stores
Some remnants of the English written scrip
We left with baby; then we called him lost,
And gave up e'en the last faint hope we held,
That he too had been kept a prisoner.
Then Tom and I, true, faithful brother hearts,
Struggled along through darkness and despair,
So poor and sad, we had no heart to write
Our poverty and sadness. But at last
We reinstated father in his place,
And settled all the troubles how we could.
Then, just as we were talking with some hope
Of going to America once more,
You send this brave young giant o'er the sea,
To call me father!
     Ah, you should have seen
His Grandsire kiss him. He is very old,
Is father, but he bade us all God-speed
On this our journey, and I promised him

I'd bring him back a daughter, fond and true—
You see, Heart's-best, I thought of little Prue.

On flows the tide of question and reply,
Of explanation asked and freely given;
But through it all we hear a far-off sound,
A chime of bells, slow throbbing on the air.
'Tis midnight! and beyond this mystic hour
The Sabbath and the Christmas morning lie.
To Grandsire's dim ear comes the solemn sound,
And raising his rapt, joyous, thankful eyes,
He murmurs, "Let us pray."
       Each bended knee
Touches the floor, and every eye is closed
The while his voice repeats, "Our Father blest,
Who art in Heaven, hallowed be Thy name.
Thy Kingdom come. Thy will be done on earth
As 'tis in Heaven. Give us each this day
Our daily bread. Forgive us all our sins,
And lead us not into temptation's paths,
But from all evil, oh, deliver us,
For Thine the Kingdom is, the power divine,
And Thine the glory be forevermore,
      Amen. Amen."

THE END.

NEW BOOKS

AND NEW EDITIONS,
RECENTLY ISSUED BY

G. W. CARLETON & Co., Publishers,
Madison Square, New York.

———o———

The Publishers, upon receipt of the price in advance, will send any book on this Catalogue by mail, *postage free*, to any part of the United States.

———o———

All books in this list [unless otherwise specified] are handsomely bound in cloth board binding, with gilt backs, suitable for libraries.

———o———

Mary J. Holmes' Works.

TEMPEST AND SUNSHINE............	$1 50	DARKNESS AND DAYLIGHT.........	$1 50
ENGLISH ORPHANS.................	1 50	HUGH WORTHINGTON.............	1 50
HOMESTEAD ON THE HILLSIDE......	1 50	CAMERON PRIDE..................	1 50
'LENA RIVERS....................	1 50	ROSE MATHER....................	1 50
MEADOW BROOK...................	1 50	ETHELYN'S MISTAKE..............	1 50
DORA DEANE......................	1 50	MILLBANK........................	1 50
COUSIN MAUDE....................	1 50	EDNA BROWNING......(new).......	1 50
MARIAN GRAY.....................	1 50		

Marion Harland's Works.

ALONE...........................	$1 50	SUNNYBANK.......................	$1 50
HIDDEN PATH.....................	1 50	HUSBANDS AND HOMES............	1 50
MOSS SIDE.......................	1 50	RUBY'S HUSBAND.................	1 50
NEMESIS.........................	1 50	PHEMIE'S TEMPTATION...........	1 50
MIRIAM..........................	1 50	THE EMPTY HEART................	1 50
AT LAST.........................	1 50	TRUE AS STEEL......(new).......	1 50
HELEN GARDNER...................	1 50		

Charles Dickens' Works.
"Carleton's New Illustrated Edition."

THE PICKWICK PAPERS.............	$1 50	MARTIN CHUZZLEWIT..............	$1 50
OLIVER TWIST....................	1 50	OUR MUTUAL FRIEND..............	1 50
DAVID COPPERFIELD...............	1 50	TALE OF TWO CITIES.............	1 50
GREAT EXPECTATIONS..............	1 50	CHRISTMAS BOOKS................	1 50
DOMBEY AND SON..................	1 50	SKETCHES BY "BOZ"..............	1 50
BARNABY RUDGE...................	1 50	HARD TIMES, etc................	1 50
NICHOLAS NICKLEBY...............	1 50	PICTURES OF ITALY, etc.........	1 50
OLD CURIOSITY SHOP..............	1 50	UNCOMMERCIAL TRAVELLER........	1 50
BLEAK HOUSE.....................	1 50	EDWIN DROOD, etc...............	1 50
LITTLE DORRIT...................	1 50	MISCELLANIES...................	1 50

Augusta J. Evans' Novels.

BEULAH..........................	$1 75	ST. ELMO........................	$2 00
MACARIA.........................	1 75	VASHTI......(new)...............	2 00
INEZ............................	1 75		

Captain Mayne Reid — Illustrated.

SCALP HUNTERS	$1 50	WHITE CHIEF	$1 50
WAR TRAIL	1 50	HEADLESS HORSEMAN	1 50
HUNTER'S FEAST	1 50	LOST LENORE	1 50
TIGER HUNTER	1 50	WOOD RANGERS	1 50
OSCEOLA, THE SEMINOLE	1 50	WILD HUNTRESS	1 50
THE QUADROON	1 50	THE MAROON	1 50
RANGERS AND REGULATORS	1 50	RIFLE RANGERS	1 50
WHITE GAUNTLET	1 50	WILD LIFE	1 50

A. S. Roe's Works.

A LONG LOOK AHEAD	$1 50	TRUE TO THE LAST	$1 50
TO LOVE AND TO BE LOVED	1 50	LIKE AND UNLIKE	1 50
TIME AND TIDE	1 50	LOOKING AROUND	1 50
I'VE BEEN THINKING	1 50	WOMAN OUR ANGEL	1 50
THE STAR AND THE CLOUD	1 50	THE CLOUD ON THE HEART	1 50
HOW COULD HE HELP IT	1 50	RESOLUTION (new)	1 50

Hand-Books of Society.

THE HABITS OF GOOD SOCIETY. The nice points of taste and good manners, and the art of making oneself agreeable.....................$1 75
THE ART OF CONVERSATION.—A sensible work, for every one who wishes to be either an agreeable talker or listener............................ 1 50
THE ARTS OF WRITING, READING, AND SPEAKING.—An excellent book for self-instruction and improvement.................................... 1 50
A NEW DIAMOND EDITION of the above three popular books.—Small size, elegantly bound, and put in a box.............................. 3 00

Mrs. Hill's Cook Book.

MRS. A. P. HILL'S NEW COOKERY BOOK, and family domestic receipts..........$2 00

Miss Muloch's Novels.

JOHN HALIFAX, GENTLEMAN......$1 75 | A LIFE FOR A LIFE.............$1 75

Charlotte Bronte [Currer Bell].

JANE EYRE—a novel............$1 75 | SHIRLEY—a novel................$1 75

Louisa M. Alcott.

MORNING GLORIES—A beautiful juvenile, by the author of "Little Women".....1 50

The Crusoe Books—Famous "Star Edition."

ROBINSON CRUSOE.—New illustrated edition....................................$1 50
SWISS FAMILY ROBINSON.   Do.   Do 1 50
THE ARABIAN NIGHTS.   Do.   Do 1 50

Julie P. Smith's Novels.

WIDOW GOLDSMITH'S DAUGHTER	$1 75	THE WIDOWER	$1 75
CHRIS AND OTHO	1 75	THE MARRIED BELLE	1 75
TEN OLD MAIDS.. [in press]	1 75		

Artemus Ward's Comic Works.

ARTEMUS WARD—HIS BOOK	$1 50	ARTEMUS WARD—IN LONDON	$1 50
ARTEMUS WARD—HIS TRAVELS	1 50	ARTEMUS WARD—HIS PANORAMA	1 50

Fanny Fern's Works.

FOLLY AS IT FLIES	$1 50	CAPER-SAUCE ......(new)	$1 50
GINGERSNAPS	1 50		

Josh Billings' Comic Works.

JOSH BILLINGS' PROVERBS........$1 50 | JOSH BILLINGS FARMER'S ALMINAX, 25 cts
JOSH BILLINGS ON ICE............ 1 50 | (In paper covers.)

Verdant Green.

A racy English college story—with numerous comic illustrations..............$1 50

Popular Italian Novels.

DOCTOR ANTONIO.—A love story of Italy. By Ruffini...................$1 75
BEATRICE CENCI.—By Guerrazzi. With a steel Portrait..................... 1 75

M. Michelet's Remarkable Works.

LOVE (L'AMOUR).—English translation from the original French.............$1 50
WOMAN (LA FEMME).   Do.   Do.   Do 1 50

G. W. CARLETON & CO.'S PUBLICATIONS.

Ernest Renan's French Works.
THE LIFE OF JESUS .... $1 75 | LIFE OF SAINT PAUL $1 75
LIVES OF THE APOSTLES .... 1 75 | BIBLE IN INDIA. By Jacolliot 2 00

Geo. W. Carleton.
OUR ARTIST IN CUBA.—With 50 comic illustrations of life and customs $1 50
OUR ARTIST IN PERU.   Do.   Do.   Do. 1 50
OUR ARTIST IN AFRICA. (In press)   Do.   Do. 1 50

May Agnes Fleming's Novels.
GUY EARLESCOURT'S WIFE .... $1 75 | A WONDERFUL WOMAN. (In press). $1 75

Maria J. Westmoreland's Novels.
HEART HUNGRY .... $1 75 | CLIFFORD TROUP ..... (new) $1 75

Sallie A. Brock's Novels.
KENNETH, MY KING .... $1 75 | A NEW BOOK ...... (in press) ......

Author of "Rutledge."
RUTLEDGE.—A novel .... $1 50 | LOUIE.—A novel $1 50

Victor Hugo.
LES MISERABLES.—English translation from the French. Octavo $2 50
LES MISERABLES.—In the Spanish language 5 00

Algernon Charles Swinburne.
LAUS VENERIS, AND OTHER POEMS.—An elegant new edition $1 50
FRENCH LOVE-SONGS.—Selected from the best French authors 1 50

Robert Dale Owen.
THE DEBATABLE LAND BETWEEN THIS WORLD AND THE NEXT $2 00

Guide for New York City.
WOOD'S ILLUSTRATED HAND-BOOK.—A beautiful pocket volume ....

The Game of Whist.
POLE ON WHIST.—The late English standard work $1 00

Mansfield T. Walworth's Novels.
WARWICK .... $1 75 | STORMCLIFF $1 75
LULU .... 1 75 | DELAPLAINE 1 75
HOTSPUR .... 1 75 | BEVERLY ...... (new) 1 75
A NEW NOVEL ...... (in press) ......

Mother Goose Set to Music.
MOTHER GOOSE MELODIES.—With music for singing, and illustrations $1 50

Tales from the Operas.
THE PLOTS OF POPULAR OPERAS in the form of stories $1 50

M. M. Pomeroy "Brick."
SENSE—(a serious book) .... $1 50 | NONSENSE—(a comic book) $1 50
GOLD-DUST   do.   .... 1 50 | BRICK-DUST   do. 1 50
OUR SATURDAY NIGHTS .... 1 50 | LIFE OF M. M POMEROY 1 50

John Esten Cooke's Works.
FAIRFAX .... $1 50 | HAMMER AND RAPIER $1 50
HILT TO HILT .... 1 50 | OUT OF THE FOAM 1 50
A NEW BOOK ...... (in press) ......

Joseph Rodman Drake.
THE CULPRIT FAY.—The well-known faery poem, with 100 illustrations $2 00
THE CULPRIT FAY.   Do.   superbly bound in turkey morocco .. 5 00

Richard B. Kimball's Works.
WAS HE SUCCESSFUL? .... $1 75 | LIFE IN SAN DOMINGO $1 50
UNDERCURRENTS OF WALL STREET. 1 75 | HENRY POWERS, BANKER 1 75
SAINT LEGER .... 1 75 | TO-DAY 1 75
ROMANCE OF STUDENT LIFE .... 1 75 | EMILIE ...... (in press) ....

Author "New Gospel of Peace."
CHRONICLES OF GOTHAM.—A rich modern satire (paper covers) .... 25 cts.
THE FALL OF MAN.—A satire on the Darwin theory do.   .... 50 cts.

Celia E. Gardner's Novels.
STOLEN WATERS .... $1 50 | BROKEN DREAMS $1 50

4   G. W. CARLETON & CO.'S PUBLICATIONS.

Edmund Kirke's Works.

AMONG THE PINES.................$1 50	ADRIFT IN DIXIE..................$1 50
MY SOUTHERN FRIENDS............ 1 50	AMONG THE GUERILLAS............ 1 50
DOWN IN TENNESSEE............... 1 50	

Dr. Cumming's Works.

THE GREAT TRIBULATION..........$2 00	TEACH US TO PRAY...............$2 00
THE GREAT PREPARATION......... 2 00	LAST WARNING CRY............... 2 00
THE GREAT CONSUMMATION....... 2 00	THE SEVENTH VIAL............... 2 00

Stephe Smith.

ROMANCE AND HUMOR OF THE RAILROAD.—Illustrated........................$1 50

Plymouth Church,—Brooklyn.

A HISTORY OF THIS CHURCH ; from 1847 to 1873.—Illustrated..............$2 00

Orpheus C. Kerr.

O. C. KERR PAPERS.—4 vols. in 1...$2 00	THE CLOVEN FOOT.—A novel.....$1 50
AVERY GLIBUN.—A novel........... 2 00	SMOKED GLASS. Do. 1 50

Miscellaneous Works.

BRAZEN GATES.—A juvenile.......$1 50	CHRISTMAS HOLLY.—Marion Harland$1 50
ANTIDOTE TO GATES AJAR........ 25 cts	DREAM MUSIC.—F. R. Marvin...... 1 50
THE RUSSIAN BALL (paper)...... 25 cts	POEMS.—By L. G. Thomas........ 1 50
THE SNOBLACE BALL do ...... 25 cts	VICTOR HUGO.—His life.......... 2 00
DEAFNESS.—Dr. E. B. Lighthill.... 1 00	BEAUTY IS POWER................ 1 50
A BOOK ABOUT LAWYERS.......... 2 00	PASTIMES, with little friends...... 1 50
A BOOK ABOUT DOCTORS......... 2 00	WOMAN, LOVE, AND MARRIAGE..... 1 50
GOLDEN CROSS.—Irving Van Wart.. 1 50	WILL-'O-THE-WISP.—A juvenile..... 1 50
PRISON-LIFE OF JEFFERSON DAVIS .. 2 00	WICKEDEST WOMAN in New York.. 25 cts
RAMBLES IN CUBA................ 1 50	COUNSEL FOR GIRLS.............. 1 50
SQUIBOB PAPERS.—John Phœnix.... 1 50	SANDWICHES.—ArtemusWard (pa'r) 25 cts
WIDOW SPRIGGINS.—Widow Bedott. 1 75	

Miscellaneous Novels.

MARK GILDERSLEEVE.—J. S. Sauzade$1 75	FAUSTINA.—From the German.....$1 50
FERNANDO DE LEMOS............. 2 00	MAURICE.—From the French....... 1 50
CROWN JEWELS.—Mrs. Moffatt.... 1 75	GUSTAVE ADOLF.—From the Swedish 1 50
A LOST LIFE.—Emily Moore....... 1 50	ADRIFT WITH A VENGEANCE....... 1 50
ROBERT GREATHOUSE.—J. F. Swift. 2 00	UP BROADWAY.—Eleanor Kirk.... 1 50
ATHALIAH.—J. H. Greene, Jr..... 1 75	MONTALBAN...................... 1 75
FOUR OAKS.—Kamba Thorpe...... 1 75	LIFE AND DEATH 1 50
PROMETHEUS IN ATLANTIS........ 2 00	JARGAL.—By Victor Hugo......... 1 50
TITAN........................... 2 00	CLAUDE GNEUX.—By Victor Hugo.. 1 50
COUSIN PAUL.................... 1 75	THE HONEYMOON.—A love story.... 1 50
VANQUISHED.—Agnes Leonard.. .. 1 75	MARY BRANDEGEE.—Cuyler Pine... 1 75
MERQUEM.—George Sand......... 1 75	RENSHAWE.—Cuyler Pine.......... 1 75

Miscellaneous Works.

A BOOK OF EPITAPHS.—Amusing, quaint, and curious......(new)............$1 50
WOMEN AND THEATRES.—A sketchy book by Olive Logan.............. 1 50
SOUVENIRS OF TRAVEL.—By Madame Octavia Walton LeVert............... 2 00
THE ART OF AMUSING.—A book of home amusements, with numerous illustrations, 1 50
HOW TO MAKE MONEY ; and how to keep it.—T. A. Davies................... 1 50
ITALIAN LIFE ; and Legend.—Anna Cora Mowatt. Illustrated............. 1 50
BALLAD OF LORD BATEMAN.—Illustrations by Cruikshank (paper)... .... 25 cts
ANGELINA GUSHINGTON.—Thoughts on men and things................... 1 50
BEHIND THE SCENES ; at the "White House."—By Elizabeth Keckley........ 2 00
THE YACHTMAN'S PRIMER.—For amateur sailors. T. R. Warren (paper)...... 50 cts
RURAL ARCHITECTURE.—By M. Field. With plans and illustrations.......... 2 00
LIFE OF HORACE GREELEY.—By L. U. Reavis. With Portrait................ 2 00
WHAT I KNOW OF FARMING.—By Horace Greeley......................... 1 50
THE FRANCO-PRUSSIAN WAR IN 1870.—By M. D. Landon. With maps........ 2 00
PRACTICAL TREATISE ON LABOR.—By Hendrick B. Wright.................... 2 00
TWELVE VIEWS OF HEAVEN.—By Distinguished Divines...................... 1 50
HOUSES NOT MADE WITH HANDS.—An illustrated juvenile, illustrated by Hoppin 1 00
LIVING WRITERS OF THE SOUTH.—By Professor J. W. Davidson............ 2 00
CRUISE OF THE ALABAMA AND SUMTER.—By Captain Semmes 1 50
NOJOQUE.—A question for a continent. By H. R. Helper.................. 2 00
IMPENDING CRISIS OF THE SOUTH.   Do. 2 00
NEGROES IN NEGROLAND.   Do.   (paper)............. 1 00

www.ingramcontent.com/pod-product-compliance
Lightning Source LLC
Chambersburg PA
CBHW020918230426
43666CB00008B/1484